FAITH
in the
CRISIS

REV. DR. ADRIAN SMITH

WESTBOW
PRESS®
A DIVISION OF THOMAS NELSON
& ZONDERVAN

This book is a work of non-fiction. Unless otherwise noted, the author and the publisher make no explicit guarantees as to the accuracy of the information contained in this book and in some cases, names of people and places have been altered to protect their privacy.

Unless otherwise indicated, scripture quotations are taken from the NRSV (New Revised Standard Version Bible), copyright 1989, Division of Christian Education of the National Council of the Churches of Christ in the United States of America. Used by permission. All rights reserved."

Scripture quotations marked (NLT) are taken from the Holy Bible, New Living Translation, copyright ©1996, 2004, 2015 by Tyndale House Foundation. Used by permission of Tyndale House Publishers, a Division of Tyndale House Ministries, Carol Stream, Illinois 60188. All rights reserved.

WestBow Press books may be ordered through booksellers or by contacting:

WestBow Press
A Division of Thomas Nelson & Zondervan
1663 Liberty Drive
Bloomington, IN 47403
www.westbowpress.com
844-714-3454

Because of the dynamic nature of the Internet, any web addresses or links contained in this book may have changed since publication and may no longer be valid. The views expressed in this work are solely those of the author and do not necessarily reflect the views of the publisher, and the publisher hereby disclaims any responsibility for them.

Cover photo by The Morgan Media

Any people depicted in stock imagery provided by Getty Images are models, and such images are being used for illustrative purposes only. Certain stock imagery © Getty Images.

ISBN: 979-8-3850-1325-8 (sc)
ISBN: 979-8-3850-1326-5 (e)

Library of Congress Control Number: 2023922381

Print information available on the last page.

WestBow Press rev. date: 12/21/2023

FAITH IN THE CRISIS

As the COVID-19 pandemic ravaged the world, the Spirit of God gave me some clear directives. Among the most resonant of these spiritual directives was the call to actively and specifically encourage faith and hope. This culminated in two sets of sermon series leading to the rebranding of Sunday morning services as "**Moments of Hope**," which form the core of this work.

The journey to this publication was not straightforward. Members like Alfred King would consistently challenge and encourage me to publish my sermons, to put pen to paper. For a time, I resisted. Initially, doubts about my own capability held me back. Later, internal struggles became obstacles. With the daunting responsibility of pastoring three churches, serving on my denomination's regional leadership board, and managing other duties, the idea of writing or publishing seemed unfeasible.

However, about a year after the first Covid-19 case was reported in Barbados, a conversation with a congregation member illuminated the broader impact of my sermons. She recounted the positive influence my words from the past year had on her family, especially her mother. This member inquired if I had considered compiling my sermons into a book, thinking of those who might not be on social media platforms. She would have been surprised to know that the title of such a book, along with its incomplete chapters, already resided on a flash drive in my office.

In that moment, I felt a deep conviction from the Spirit. What follows in these pages are words inspired by God's Holy Spirit, intended to provide solace and encouragement through any crisis you might be confronting.

God's words comforted me, fortified me, enabling not just survival but resilience through the pandemic. They empowered me to shepherd God's flock during one of the most tumultuous epochs in modern history. This journey has underlined the crucial role of faith, especially when circumstances deteriorate, and the invaluable blessing of unwavering belief against overwhelming odds. My earnest prayer is that this book galvanizes your faith in God as you navigate your own crises.

CONTENTS

Dedication

I dedicate this work to my parents, Juliette Smith, Reginald and Judy Smith, and to my spiritual mom, Rev. Lillette I George, who modelled not just talking faith, but living by faith.

ACKNOWLEDGMENTS

- To God the Redeemer and Sustainer of my life. It is in You, God, that I live and move and have my entire being.
- To my wife, Andrea, and my family, whose love and support continues to be the balance in my life.
- To the team of Rev. TG Morrison, Rev. Winston Jones, Simone Cumberbatch, Cheryl C. Harewood and Carol David Kendall whose eyes and critiques have shaped this beautiful work.
- To Mrs. Stacia Mascoll; God's timing is perfect, and your guidance throughout this process has been invaluable.
- To the wonderful Moravian congregations of Calvary, Gracehill and Fulnec, and by extension, the Moravian Church Barbados Conference as well as the people of God across the world who listened to the original sermons and offered insights into how God spoke to you.
- To you reading this work, thank you!

FOREWORD

You hold in your hand a work of excellence. **Faith In The Crisis** is no ordinary book. It is a work of excellence which, will cause you to search deep down in your heart and after much inner reflection, cause you to reconsider your Christian walk. Are you truly walking in the Spirt? Have you allowed your trials, tests and challenges to increase your faith in God? What about navigating through the COVID-19 pandemic? Have you personally discovered the positives derived from this global battle which took the lives of many, and no doubt, caused the faith of countless others to increase? If you are a pastor, missionary, a worship leader, congregant, a child and servant of God in any way, have you allowed the lessons from COVID-19 to catapult you into being a better ambassador for Christ? If you have not, this book will show you how to.

You also hold in your hand a book from a respected preacher, husband, father, son and pastor. It is a book which will cause you to pause and think; a book which will take you on a beautiful spirit-led, spirit-filled journey.

To have become affiliated with Reverend Dr. Adrian Smith who, has been a leader in the Moravian Church for the past 21 years, is to have become acquainted with a genuine, committed minister of the Gospel; one to whom God has entrusted the delivery and preaching of His Word, and given the task to shepherd His people, both of which he does with a sense of humility and abiding faith.

Reverend Dr. Adrian Smith, an advocate for truth, has written **Faith In The Crisis** at a time when constant changes in a changing world propel us to draw closer to God who is the Author and Finisher of our faith.

May this book excite you into trusting God more, and may it strengthen you in your walk with Him.

Happy reading.

Pastor Cheryl C. Harewood,
church leader, author and journalist

PREFACE

In the epic biblical book of Job, the pre-patriarchal figure Job while wrestling with theodicy, was forced to make this unnerving observation: "A mortal born of a woman, few of days and full of trouble, comes up like a flower and withers, flees like a shadow and does not last." Job 14:1-2 NRSV. Therefore, like an ancient sage, he sought to impress upon his readers a timeless truth; that intrinsically woven in the DNA of all human beings is the capacity to adapt and adjust to crises (troubles) as they are a part of mortals lived reality and beyond mortal's control. How crises are handled exposes one's character, maturity and spirituality.

Those who profess faith in Jesus of Nazareth-God's Christ ought to be characterized by a living faith while standing boldly in the Faith, hence a justification for the nomenclature 'Believers'. So, notwithstanding the crises, Believers confront them with fortitude assured that: "The Lord of hosts is with us, the God of Jacob is our refuge." (Psalm 46:7 NRSV) and that all will work for the good.

Without question, the recent global pandemic as a direct result of the contagious pathology of the COVID-19 Virus, exposed those who were faith-filled and faithful. While many faced the temptation to succumb to fear or adopt the agenda of powerful entities, believers were challenged to take seriously the

Prophet Habakkuk's admonition: "but the righteous shall live by their faith." (Habakkuk 2:4, NRSV). Many Believers were determined to trust the God they served before COVID-19 during COVID-19 and were not disappointed.

During the pandemic a few pastoral and prophetic voices could be heard blaring 'like trumpets in the dark' directing all and sundry to the tranquil 'river of God'. One such Nabi is the Rev Dr. Adrian R. Smith, who intentionally summoned believers to focus on the God in the midst of the crises and not merely upon the crises. Weekly through kerygma, believers were urged to allow their faith to seek understanding and to discern what God in Christ Spirit was speaking to the churches.

Now, these insights, initially shared in one small part of God's vineyard are being made available to the wider 'Body of Christ' in the form of a book. By employing the exegetical tools and acutely aware of the social realities Rev Dr. Adrian Smith has produced a work that offers powerful perspectives, practical principles and priceless pronouncements. Skillfully engaging in critical hermeneutics, Rev. Smith fused the lyrics of popular hymns, songs and choruses to help non-ordained Believers understand otherwise lofty concepts. Page after page rivets the reader as their spiritual thirst is slaked and their souls fed with heavenly manna. The reader is brought to at least two impregnable truths: Jesus the Christ is the SOURCE OF FAITH and THE AUTHOR AND FINISHER OF PERFECTER OF OUR FAITH.

For those who are in active Christian Ministry, the last chapter is like an oasis in the desert. Contained therein is a tremendous fount of encouragement provided for those meandering through the labyrinth of Christian Ministry in anti-theistic 21st century world and feeling weary, worried and wounded. The evidence is overwhelming and strongly asserts, those who lead other to faith must themselves with joy draw from the wellsprings of salvation.

Finally, it is my prayer that all who ingest and digest these sermons, be spiritually stimulated to live by faith as they live out the Faith. Fully cognizant that, at the Second Advent of Christ, the existential question that will be asked to settle all things: "...will He find faith on earth?" Luke 18:8c NRSV. Thank God, this book anchored in God in Christ's immutable WORD, aids in the ultimate answer being a resounding YES!

Seeking to be faith-filled and faithful,
Rev. T. G. Morrison
Senior Pastor Zion Baptist Church
The Bahamas

INTRODUCTION
IN TIMES OF CRISIS

In today's world, humanity finds itself amidst multifaceted crises. The pandemic is still going strong, economic terms like "recession" and "depression" are now commonplace, and geopolitical tensions, like the conflict between Russia and Ukraine, Israel and Palestine exacerbate global instability. Yet, the common refrain we hear is that these are "unprecedented times."

Beyond COVID-19, a myriad of challenges prevail. From natural calamities like hurricanes, landslides, and volcanic eruptions to societal issues such as civil unrest, many worldwide face adversity. Personal challenges, whether medical or familial, strike even closer to home. In this tapestry of turmoil, whether personal, national, or global, the thread of crises remains constant. The pressing need for unwavering faith is palpable.

Carey Nieuwhof insightfully observed that "A crisis acts as an accelerator." Trends emerging pre-pandemic, notably the rise of post-Christian culture, gained momentum. John Maxwell encapsulates a crisis as a pivotal moment demanding a resolute decision. The choice to trust God in times characterized by upheaval and uncertainty stands paramount.

Faith in the Crisis navigates these turbulent waters, offering direction and solace through biblical tales. The pandemic introduced three major societal shifts such as lockdowns, social distancing, and mask mandates, underscoring the essence of unyielding trust in God for believers.

Because of COVID-19: A three-part series conceived in the wake of Barbados's Prime Minister's announcement of a second lockdown. It is a testament to faith in the face of adversity.

A Call To Trust God In Difficult Times draws on the profound life experiences of biblical legends like Elijah, Job, David, the woman with the issue of blood, and most certainly, the transformative figure of Jesus the One who walked among us.

Moments of Hope calls us to have resilience and to reshape ministry in these changing times.

BECAUSE OF COVID 19

LOCKED DOWN BUT NOT LOCKED OUT

Acts 16:22-34

²² The crowd joined in attacking them, and the magistrates had them stripped of their clothing and ordered them to be beaten with rods. ²³ After they had given them a severe flogging, they threw them into prison and ordered the jailer to keep them securely. ²⁴ Following these instructions, he put them in the innermost cell and fastened their feet in the stocks.

²⁵ About midnight Paul and Silas were praying and singing hymns to God, and the prisoners were listening to them. ²⁶ Suddenly there was an earthquake, so violent that the foundations of the prison were shaken; and immediately all the doors were opened and everyone's chains were unfastened. ²⁷ When the jailer woke up and saw the prison doors wide open, he drew his sword and was about to

kill himself, since he supposed that the prisoners had escaped. [28] But Paul shouted in a loud voice, "Do not harm yourself, for we are all here." [29] The jailer[e] called for lights, and rushing in, he fell down trembling before Paul and Silas. [30] Then he brought them outside and said, "Sirs, what must I do to be saved?" [31] They answered, "Believe on the Lord Jesus, and you will be saved, you and your household." [32] They spoke the word of the Lord[f] to him and to all who were in his house. [33] At the same hour of the night he took them and washed their wounds; then he and his entire family were baptized without delay. [34] He brought them up into the house and set food before them; and he and his entire household rejoiced that he had become a believer in God.

In March of 2020, the world grappled with a pandemic that redefined many aspects of daily life. Barbados, like many other nations, introduced a national lockdown. The ramifications were immediately felt by everyone: in-person worship was suspended, eliminating the chance for believers to attend special Christian calendar services like Palm Sunday, Good Friday, and Easter Sunday. Popular fast-food restaurants, gyms, barbers, and hairdressers all closed their doors. Travel was restricted to essential trips only, putting an end to shopping excursions and sight-seeing. It felt as if Barbados, and indeed the world, had come to an abrupt halt. Working from home became the norm, and education shifted online.

Before 2020, the term "lockdown" primarily conjured images of prisoners confined to their cells. Today, the term has taken on a broader meaning. It refers to an emergency protocol prohibiting movement due to imminent danger, often from a severe disease outbreak. Now, "lockdown" represents a temporary state where people, under governmental guidelines, limit their outside activities to prevent disease spread.

Amidst the pandemic, many grappled with feelings of fear and frustration due to altered social scenarios. However, it's crucial to understand that while our physical movements might be constrained, our spiritual essence remains unfettered. I remind you that a physical lockdown does not mean a spiritual lockdown.

Physical Lockdown DOES NOT Mean A Spiritual Lockdown!

God is still at work, even in a lockdown. Our movement might be restricted but The Holy Spirit of God is not restricted. No physical barrier can bind the Holy Spirit. Despite any lockdown or restriction, God continues His divine work. He is not confined by time or space, and no worldly lockdown can prevent His Spirit from bringing healing, touch, and transformative change.

Such moments of stillness and restriction can, paradoxically, be fertile grounds for spiritual growth. Consider the biblical account of Paul and Silas. Their incarceration wasn't in a comfortable, modern-day jail with internet, a flat-screen TV and air conditioning, but rather in a dark, cold cell, likely reeking of decay. Their captivity, in the innermost chamber, was a symbolic representation of a place devoid of hope or rescue. Moreover, they endured the agony of stocks, likely stretching their limbs to painful extremes making movement difficult and uncomfortable. Yet, even in such despairing conditions, they found spiritual liberation.

Many times, we might feel similarly "imprisoned" in life, trapped in routines or painful situations, in painful physical places seemingly with no forward momentum. Yet, even in those trying moments, remember that while you may be physically confined or "locked down," you are never spiritually "locked out" from the solace of prayer.

1. Lockdown But Not Locked Out From Prayer

25 About midnight Paul and Silas were praying and singing hymns to God, and the prisoners were listening to them.

Prayer is a spiritual discipline that transcends the confines of place and time. While certain locations might traditionally be associated with this divine connection, communion, and conversation, the essence of prayer remains unaffected by our surroundings.

Consider the story of Paul and Silas in verse 16. Their journey to a designated place of prayer was interrupted, leading them to prison. Yet, confinement didn't deter their spirit. Just as Paul and Silas continued their dialogue with God from the confines of a cell, we too can turn any space into sacred ground — be it our home, car, or even a momentary retreat to a quiet corner during work.

Pray in your bedroom, bathroom, living room, dining room, garage, car, patio, or while walking around your home. Don't get too caught up on the specific place of prayer. Pay more attention to the act of praying which, can occur anywhere and at any time. At about midnight, Paul and Silas were singing and praying.

We often reserve specific times or ceremonies for prayer, be it a morning ritual, a quick word of gratitude before meals or even bedtime prayers such as one I learnt as a child, ***"Now I lay me down to sleep, I pray the Lord my soul to keep. If I should die before I wake, I pray the Lord my soul to take."***

However, there are moments when life's challenges urge us to reach out to God— perhaps in the stillness of the night, before significant life events, or even in daily moments of introspection.

Interestingly, the term "praying" translates to "proseuchomai" in Greek, indicating a wish or desire. This definition aligns beautifully with the essence of prayer, where we present our hopes and yearnings to God. It brings to mind the hymn Sweet Hour of Prayer, which encourages us to make all our "wants and wishes known," capturing the essence of what it truly means to pray.

Sweet hour of prayer! Sweet hour of prayer!
That calls me from a world of care
And bids me at my Father's throne
Make all my wants and wishes known.
In seasons of distress and grief
My soul has often found relief
And oft escaped the tempter's snare,
By thy return, sweet hour of prayer!

Sweet hour of prayer! Sweet hour of prayer!
Thy wings shall my petition bear
To Him whose truth and faithfulness
Engage the waiting soul to bless.
And since He bids me seek His face

Believe His Word and trust His grace
I'll cast on Him my every care
And wait for thee, sweet hour of prayer!

Text: Attributed to William W. Walford, 1772–1850, alt.Music: William B. Bradbury, 1816–1868, alt.

We find another dimension that profoundly impacts our conversation with God: **Boldness**. 1 John 5:14 – 15 enlightens us on this:

> **14 And this is the boldness we have in him, that if we ask anything according to his will, he hears us. 15 And if we know that he hears us in whatever we ask, we know that we have obtained the requests made of him.**

What does it mean to pray with boldness? It's more than just the absence of fear. Boldness in prayer is an act of spiritual courage, a testament to our unwavering faith and trust in God. It signifies our willingness to embrace His will, even when the path forward seems uncertain. Think of it as a child confidently asking a loving parent, not fearing rejection but trusting in unconditional love.

As Paul reminds us, God hasn't endowed us with timidity, God has not given us a spirit of fear, but a spirit of power, love, and self-discipline. This spirit fuels our bold prayers. When we bravely ask in alignment with God's purpose, we're assured of His attentive ear. It is Spirit-led courage.

In the confines of a lockdown, while many doors may close, the gateway to God through prayer remains wide open. And with boldness, we can step through, knowing that we might be physically confined, but spiritually, we're as free as ever.

2. We Are Lockdown But Not Locked Out From Praise

Despite the bars of confinement, our souls have wings of praise. In Acts 16:25, we read: "About midnight Paul and Silas were praying and singing hymns to God."

Luke's choice of the imperfect tense in the Greek, describing their actions, paints a vivid picture. It reveals that Paul and Silas started their songs of praise in the past, and they perpetuated this song, unfazed by their shackled state. It's as if they're urging us to praise God before the lockdown, praise Him during, and continue in the aftermath.

Our adulations serve a dual purpose – they are both about God and for God. Job's unwavering dedication, even amid unimaginable trials, stands as a testament. When Satan challenges Job's faith, suggesting he worships God only during fair weather **("Skin for skin! All that the man has he will give for his life. 5 But stretch out your hand now and touch his bone and his flesh, and he will curse you to your face. Job 2:4-5),** we're prompted to introspect. Is that true about us? Are our songs of praise conditional, convenient, and sung only in the sunshine of life? Do we only praise God when our prayers are answered, and the blessings are flowing in abundance? Or, can our voices soar even when the clouds gather, through the hurt, the pain, the sickness and while we are waiting for prayers to be answered?

Paul and Silas exemplified this. Their hymns echoed in the heart of midnight, a symbolic period representing the darkest, most challenging phase, when we are tired, weary, sleepy and low. They weren't just confined in any part of the prison but in the innermost cell, where light barely pierced (the darkest hour (midnight) and the darkest space (innermost cell). Amid potential filth, untreated wounds, and shackled feet, their spirit remained unbroken. It's almost as if their dire circumstances amplified their songs, a resonant declaration of faith.

So, let this be an inspiration. Whether you're weathering personal, financial, or emotional storms, let your heart be your sanctuary. And from that sacred space, let your praises rise, let them rise from the inside. Your physical space might feel confining, but your spirit knows no bounds. In every challenge, find a note of gratitude and a song of praise. Sing, for God is always listening.

[25] About midnight Paul and Silas were praying and singing hymns to God."

This narrative isn't about exalting hymns over choruses or contemporary songs. Delving into the Greek, hýmnos (originating from hydeō, "to celebrate") means a celebratory song. Its core purpose is to honor, praise, and give thanks. Whether it's a hymn, chorus, or contemporary melody, what's paramount is its homage to the Almighty God. And the beauty lies in the authenticity; it doesn't need to be harmonious or pitch-perfect. A joyful noise is all that's required. Take that from someone who didn't think he could sing well but hasn't stopped praising the Lord. Let's all be encouraged to vocalize our faith.

Ephesians 5:18 – 20(NLT) beautifully conveys this: "... be filled with the Holy Spirit, [19] singing psalms and hymns and spiritual songs among yourselves, and making music to the Lord in your hearts. [20] And give thanks for everything to God the Father in the name of our Lord Jesus Christ.

Similarly, Colossians 3:16 urges: "Let the word of Christ dwell in you richly; teach and admonish one another in all wisdom; and with gratitude in your hearts sing psalms, hymns, and spiritual songs to God."

The story is told about Civilla Martin, born in 1866 in Nova Scotia, who became a beacon of faith. Together with her evangelist husband, they traversed the U.S., enriching lives with their evangelistic campaigns. Yet, it's a visit to a bedridden friend that truly inspired Civilla. Amid her friend's physical ailment was unwavering faith, a belief that the same God watching over the sparrows was watching over her. This profound realization led Civilla to pen a poignant poem, encapsulating this moving experience. She completed it the same day.[1]

"Why should I feel discouraged, why should the shadows come,
Why should my heart be lonely, and long for heav'n and home,
When Jesus is my portion? My constant Friend is He:
His eye is on the sparrow, and I know He watches me;
His eye is on the sparrow, and I know He watches me.

- *Refrain:*
  I sing because I'm happy, I sing because I'm free,
  For His eye is on the sparrow, and I know He watches me.

"Let not your heart be troubled," His tender word I hear,
And resting on His goodness, I lose my doubts and fears;
Though by the path He leadeth, but one step I may see;
His eye is on the sparrow, and I know He watches me;
His eye is on the sparrow, and I know He watches me.

Locked down but not locked out. We are not locked out from prayer, not locked out from praise.

3. Lockdown But Not Locked Out
From Promoting Christ

> ²⁵ **About midnight Paul and Silas were praying and singing hymns to God, and the prisoners were listening to them.**

Amidst their personal trials, Paul and Silas became unwitting evangelists. Their spiritual resilience not only comforted them but also resonated with their fellow inmates. Some biblical interpretations even suggest that the word "listening" here implies listening with pleasure. This means that these hymns and prayers, rooted in the love and teachings of Christ, found a receptive audience amongst the prisoners.

And this wasn't merely passive listening. The jailer, affected by their unwavering faith, posed a question that laid bare his spiritual thirst: "Sirs, what must I do to be saved?" To which the response was unequivocal: "Believe on the Lord Jesus, and you will be saved, you and your household." They then shared the Gospel with the jailer and his entire household, emphasizing the central role of Jesus Christ in salvation.

Such moments underline our sacred responsibility to promote Christ in our words and deeds. Irrespective of our situations, the story of Jesus—His birth, life, sacrifice, and resurrection—should be the beacon we share. The urgency of this mission is vital, for there's always someone seeking solace, searching for a savior.

A poignant moment came after the earthquake.

> ²⁷ **When the jailer woke up and saw the prison doors wide open, he drew his sword and was about to kill himself, since he supposed that the prisoners had escaped.** ²⁸

But Paul shouted in a loud voice, "Do not harm yourself, for we are all here." [29] The jailer called for lights, and rushing in, he fell down trembling before Paul and Silas. [30] Then he brought them outside and said, "Sirs, what must I do to be saved?"

The immediate response for many would be to seize this newfound freedom and flee. But not Paul and Silas. Their decision to stay after the jail doors opened wasn't just about them; it reflected their profound commitment to live out their faith authentically.

The jailer, conditioned by the severe Roman penalties for losing prisoners, was on the verge of ending his life. Yet, Paul's reassuring shout, "Do not harm yourself, for we are all here," echoed not just an immediate assurance but the profound integrity and Christ-like compassion they embodied. A Christ like compassion that offers grace even in the most embarrassing, and shameful experiences. Our actions can exhibit grace even in the face of adversity. Integrity isn't about doing what's easy or convenient; it's about standing firm in faith even when challenges arise.

This reinforces our mandate: in all situations, we must model Christ, acting as his ambassadors in a world hungry for hope. The only Jesus some people will see, is the Jesus in you and me! Thus, we must always be mindful of this profound responsibility. **[28] But Paul shouted in a loud voice, "Do not harm yourself, for we are all here."**

The unwavering faith demonstrated by Paul and Silas, evident in their prayers, songs, and actions, profoundly affected those around them. This account serves as a powerful reminder: in every situation, our behavior and choices should align with our beliefs, as we are called to model Christ, representing a beacon of hope even in seemingly hopeless moments.

Remember, you may be locked down, but you are never locked out from praying to God, praising Him, or promoting His love. May God grant you the strength to live this truth every day.

SOCIAL DISTANCING BUT SOCIALLY CONNECTED

Philippians Chapter 1:3-11

"³ I thank my God for every remembrance of you, ⁴ always in every one of my prayers for all of you, praying with joy ⁵ for your partnership in the gospel from the first day until now. ⁶ I am confident of this, that the one who began a good work in you will continue to complete[a] it until the day of Jesus Christ. ⁷ It is right for me to think this way about all of you, because I hold you in my heart,[b] for all of you are my partners in God's grace,[c] both in my imprisonment and in the defense and confirmation of the gospel. ⁸ For God is my witness, how I long for all of you with the tender affection of Christ Jesus. ⁹ And this is my prayer, that your love may overflow more and more with knowledge and full insight ¹⁰ to help you to determine what really matters, so that in the day of Christ

you may be pure and blameless, [11] having produced the harvest[d] of righteousness that comes through Jesus Christ for the glory and praise of God.

The lessons from Apostle Paul's letters to the Philippians are timeless. Even as he was distant, he expressed a deep connection, gratitude, and yearning for the community. In today's world, this sense of connection is put to the test in unexpected ways.

During a regular shopping trip to Hill's Supermarket in Roebuck Street, St. Michael, Barbados, a stark reminder of our changed world rang out as a lady exclaimed, "My man, you too close to me, move off me!" Everyone turned to see the lady taking a step away from a gentleman. She then remarked, "You ain't hear, six feet apart? You know me? We live together?" As the embarrassed man looked around, there were people pointing him to the floor signs. Public spaces, once places of casual interaction, now have guidelines cautioning against close contact.

As outlined by the Centers for Disease Control and Prevention (CDC) in the US, "social distancing" or more aptly, "physical distancing," ensures safety by maintaining distance from those not from your household. This guidance is essential, but its terminology has raised questions.

Whitney Woolard points out that "social distancing" is a conscious effort to slow disease transmission. While this is a necessary preventive measure, there is more to consider. As one US psychologist highlighted, instead of limiting social connections, we should focus on "distant socializing."

This difference between "social" and "physical" distancing is more than just semantic:

- **Social distancing** implies isolation, potentially leading to feelings of abandonment, not a part of a loving, living body of people (1 Corinthians 12:12).
- **Physical distancing** is a straightforward call to keep a safe physical gap without severing social ties.

This is a small difference in choice of words, but a huge difference in understanding, acceptance, and consequently, practice. Especially now, maintaining social bonds is of paramount importance. While "physical distancing" is the need of the hour, let's not forget the significance of social connections. As we navigate these challenging times, remember that we may be distant, but our connections remain crucial. So, even as we stay apart, let's find ways to stay together, spiritually, emotionally, and socially.

1. We Are Responsible To Each Other

The New Testament is filled with letters – Galatians, Ephesians, Colossians, and others. Paul, through these letters, expressed his deep sense of responsibility and connection. The church in Philippi stands out as they not only sent an offering but also a member, Epaphroditus, to assist Paul. Despite challenges, like Epaphroditus falling ill, the bond between Paul and the church remained strong. This sentiment is captured in verse 3 (NLT):

"Every time I think of you, I give thanks to my God."

Connect Through Communicating

In this digital age, the sentiment remains relevant. Responsibility translates to constant communication and care. The scripture captures this essence:

"If someone says, "I love God," but hates a fellow believer,[a] that person is a liar; for if we don't love people we can see, how can we love God, whom we cannot see? [21] And he has given us this command: Those who love God must also love their fellow believers.- 1 John 4:20 – 21 (NLT) We are to let people know we care. We are to check in on others. Encourage others. Pray for others. We have a responsibility to each other. It is a responsibility to love.

Today, our tools of connection have expanded: WhatsApp, Zoom, Skype, emails, and more. Yet, the heart of the message remains the same. Reach out, even if it's a simple call, email, or even an old-school letter. Remember the joy of hearing from a loved one, or seeing a friendly wave from a distance.

For somebody who is saying they are not into all that technology, **pick up the phone and call.** Yeah, I know it costs to call landline to cell, but I am responsible to you, so I might need to tell you hang up and let me call you back.

When I was in college my parents did that a lot for me. Whenever I called home, they would say, "Hang up and I will call you back." at their expense (bless God for parents).

In today's world of digital meetings, like in a men's prayer conference I attended, Pastor David Ince emphasized the human connection, urging participants to turn on their cameras. To let others witness our smiles, warmth, and support.

Our responsibility extends beyond ourselves – it's about being there, especially for those who always stand strong for others. Sometimes, the people who seem the most resilient are the ones hoping someone will ask about their day, show some interest and some love. Simply reciprocate what they constantly do.

In our actions and words, let's remember: we are responsible not just *to* each other, but *for* each other.

2. We Are Responsible For Each Other

One of the earliest stories in the Bible, that of Cain and Abel, profoundly underscores our inherent responsibility towards each other.

> "Now Abel was a keeper of sheep, and Cain a tiller of the ground. ³ In the course of time Cain brought to the Lord an offering of the fruit of the ground, ⁴ and Abel for his part brought of the firstlings of his flock, their fat portions. And the Lord had regard for Abel and his offering, ⁵ but for Cain and his offering he had no regard. So Cain was very angry, and his countenance fell. ⁶ The Lord said to Cain, "Why are you angry, and why has your countenance fallen? ⁷ If you do well, will you not be accepted? And if you do not do well, sin is lurking at the door; its desire is for you, but you must master it."
>
> ⁸ Cain said to his brother Abel, "Let us go out to the field."[a] And when they were in the field, Cain rose up against his brother Abel and killed him. ⁹ Then

17

> the Lord said to Cain, "Where is your
> brother Abel?" He said, "I do not know;
> am I my brother's keeper?" [10] And the
> Lord said, "What have you done? Listen,
> your brother's blood is crying out to me
> from the ground! Genesis 4: 2-10.

The term "keeper," or "shamar" in Hebrew, emphasizes guardianship. It is the action one would perform if watching over a garden, a flock of sheep, or a herd of cattle. In our modern context, it begs the question: Do we watch over and care for our fellow beings? Are we conscious, alert and aware of what is happening to and with them? Sometimes we are so self-absorbed in our own desires, needs and feelings, that we exclude others. The Apostle Paul reminds us in Philippians 2:4, *"Let each of you look not to your own interests, but to the interests of others."* We are capable, and it's within our power to connect and support.

Proverbs 3:27 cautions, *"Do not withhold good from those to whom it is due, when it is in your power to do it."* Our responsibility often extends beyond immediate circles, reflecting the universal message in the parable of the Good Samaritan. As we navigate these challenging times, any act of kindness and support is essential. Remember, as the famous Nike saying goes, "Just do it!"

The Prophet Isaiah beautifully portrays the fruits of our responsibility and charity: "...**If you remove the yoke from among you, the pointing of the finger, the speaking of evil,[10] if you offer your food to the hungry and satisfy the needs of the afflicted, then your light shall rise in the darkness and your gloom be like the noonday.[11] The Lord will guide you continually, and satisfy your needs** in parched places, and make your bones strong and you shall be like a watered garden, like a spring of water, whose waters never fail." Isaiah 58: 9 – 11

In times when physical closeness may be limited, our emotional and spiritual bonds must remain strong. Let's lean on prayers, a powerful tool in maintaining these relationships. Prayers connect us, making others' burdens our own, as reflected in Galatians 6:2. Whether it's frontline workers, teachers, children struggling with online school, or overwhelmed parents, let's uphold them in our prayers. And let's broaden our horizons, praying for not just our local communities but the entire world. We share this earth and its experiences; our interconnectedness is undeniable.

3. We Are Responsible With Each Other

In a world facing unprecedented challenges, the Apostle Paul's words serve as a timely reminder:

> [9] And this is my prayer, that your love may overflow more and more with knowledge and full insight [10] to help you to determine what really matters, so that in the day of Christ you may be pure and blameless, [11] having produced the harvest[a] of righteousness that comes through Jesus Christ for the glory and praise of God. (Philippians 1:9-11)

Paul's letter, read aloud to a church, speaks to us today about mutual responsibility, echoed further in Galatians 5:13-14, "...You shall love your neighbour as yourself."

Recent times have unveiled the depths of emotional turmoil many face—rising anxiety, depression, even suicidal thoughts, especially amidst younger populations. The essence isn't just about avoiding isolation but proactively seeking connection.

If overwhelmed, seek help. Prioritize rest. Remember, the emotional toll isn't just an individual's struggle—it's a collective one. It's everyone's problem: the government, parents, schools, churches, and communities. We bear responsibility not only for ourselves but alongside and with others. As a popular Barbados entertainer sings-"all ah we!"

During the pandemic, while many showed compassion, some displayed selfishness, like hoarding supplies or stealing from public places. It's a stark reminder: We are bound together in responsibility. As believers, our duty extends to safeguarding those who might lack maturity or wisdom.

As Romans 12:15 advises, we should "rejoice with those who rejoice; weep with those who weep." Our stories and experiences, both joyful and painful, ripple through our communities, reinforcing our interconnectedness and facilitates catharsis.

Though we may practice social distancing, our social connections must strengthen. Perhaps someone comes to mind right now. Take a moment, Reach out, call, text or message. Let them know that you are thinking about them; that you care about them; that you are willing to help them. Remind them of God's love, your love and your support. As we navigate these times, let's remember a profound sentiment shared by Pope Francis:

> *"Rivers do not drink their own water; trees do not eat their own fruit; the sun does not shine on itself and flowers do not spread their fragrance for themselves.*

Living for others is a rule of nature. We are all born to help each. No matter how difficult it is...Life is good when you are happy; but much better when others are happy because of you."

In an era of social distancing, our responsibility is to remain socially and emotionally connected—for, in our shared struggles, we find collective strength.

Blest be the tie that binds
our hearts in Christian love;
the fellowship of kindred minds
is like to that above.
2 Before our Father's throne
we pour our ardent prayers;
our fears, our hopes, our aims are one,
our comforts and our cares.

Lyrics: John Fawcett (1740-1817)

WEARING A MASK
BUT UNMASKING

Matthew Chapter 7:1-5, 21-29

"Do not judge, so that you may not be judged. ² For the judgment you give will be the judgment you get, and the measure you give will be the measure you get. ³ Why do you see the speck in your neighbor's eye but do not notice the log in your own eye? ⁴ Or how can you say to your neighbor, 'Let me take the speck out of your eye,' while the log is in your own eye? ⁵ You hypocrite, first take the log out of your own eye, and then you will see clearly to take the speck out of your neighbor's eye.

²¹ "Not everyone who says to me, 'Lord, Lord,' will enter the kingdom of heaven, but only the one who does the will of my Father in heaven. ²² On that day many will say to me, 'Lord, Lord, did we not prophesy in your name, and cast

out demons in your name, and do many mighty works in your name?' ²³ Then I will declare to them, 'I never knew you; go away from me, you who behave lawlessly.'

Hearers and Doers

²⁴ "Everyone, then, who hears these words of mine and acts on them will be like a wise man who built his house on rock. ²⁵ The rain fell, the floods came, and the winds blew and beat on that house, but it did not fall because it had been founded on rock. ²⁶ And everyone who hears these words of mine and does not act on them will be like a foolish man who built his house on sand. ²⁷ The rain fell, and the floods came, and the winds blew and beat against that house, and it fell—and great was its fall!"

²⁸ Now when Jesus had finished saying these words, the crowds were astounded at his teaching, ²⁹ for he taught them as one having authority and not as their scribes.

As the nation of Barbados fervently debated on the merits of vaccines since the arrival of the first batch of Oxford AstraZeneca COVID-19 vaccines on February 9, 2021, a deeper dialogue was emerging. Dr. Brian Machlachlan, in a panel facilitated by the Bethlehem Moravian Church, illuminated the unprecedented global collaboration and advancements that underscored the development of these vaccines. Yet, amidst these strides, the emphasis remained – wear your mask, a plea echoed from every corner, every advertisement, and even by the Prime Minister of Barbados. The admonition has not only altered our daily queries before leaving home but transformed a piece of protective health equipment into a daily essential, a phenomenon reflecting the teachings of Matthew 7:1-5 where we are reminded of the importance of protecting not just ourselves, but our community.

Once, we associated masks with medical professionals, environmental pollution, or as a quirk of individuals like the late Michael Jackson. Now, in a changed world, they have burgeoned into a sign of respect and care for others. This change, however, extends beyond just the physical. Much like the teachings in Matthew 7:21-29 urging us to build our house upon a rock to withstand storms, wearing a mask signifies our commitment to building a resilient community, willing to face the storm of the pandemic with unity and consideration.

The necessity of wearing a mask has been underscored by the CDC, highlighting their role as a barrier against respiratory droplets that foster the spread of COVID-19. The stark reminder here is the obligation to wear masks correctly – covering the nose and mouth snugly, acting as a fortress against the virus, embodying the true spirit of protecting oneself and others. As emphasized in a heartfelt poem by Bruce Frazer, wearing a mask correctly symbolizes a universal care for everyone, fostering a community that wins together.

However, while masks have become a beacon of protection and unity, the pandemic has also served as a crucible, unmasking deeper underlying issues within our society. This period of crises has revealed a lack of grounded faith, with many professing belief without fully placing trust in their spirituality, reminiscent of the teachings in Matthew where it is stated that not everyone who says to Jesus, "Lord, Lord," will enter the kingdom of heaven.

Furthermore, the pandemic has unveiled a startling lack of discernment and discipline when it comes to the dissemination of information and adherence to safety protocols. It is important that we receive confirmation from reliable sources and fact check information before we disseminate information. This is still extremely relevant as we live our lives.

As we navigate this transformed world, it is paramount to reflect and rectify these shortcomings, nurturing a deep-seated faith, discernment, and discipline, virtues advocated in the scripture. As we continue to wear our masks, let us also unmask the inconsistencies within us, aligning our actions and beliefs firmly with the teachings of faith, becoming embodiments of the principles laid out in Matthew 7:1-5, 21-29.

As we continue to protect ourselves and others by wearing masks, let us also unmask and confront the deeper issues within our society and ourselves, learning to embody a faith that is both spoken and lived, fostering discernment in the information age, and cultivating discipline that goes beyond the superficial. Through this dual journey of masking and unmasking, may we emerge as a community rooted in faith, wisdom, and resilience, ready to face the challenges of a post-pandemic world with a fortified spirit and united front.

Wearing A Mask But Unmasking

1. Avoid pretentiousness. Be real. Being real with yourself should usher in a space and time when you are real with others.

In these times of unprecedented challenges, being genuine has surfaced as a cornerstone to fostering trust and solidarity in our communities. More than ever, it is crucial to be real with ourselves, a process that naturally guides us to be transparent and honest with others. The term 'hypocrite' originated from ancient Greek theatres where actors would adorn oversized masks, each painted to depict the character they were portraying. This historic practice mirrors the actions of individuals who, in everyday life, mask their true selves, performing for an audience, a façade that hides their genuine feelings and beliefs.

In the current global landscape, marked significantly by the pandemic, the act of wearing a mask has transcended its physical necessity, urging us to reconsider the masks we wear in our daily lives. These masks, akin to those worn by bank robbers in movies like "Point Break" (1991) and series like "Money Heist", are often employed to conceal one's true identity, allowing for deception and impersonation. Unfortunately, these masks also shelter the shame and pretense, masking our true characters and emotions, thereby promoting dishonesty and deceit.

As we navigate these testing times, it becomes imperative to shed these masks of pretension. It's a call to each one of us to halt the act of pretending, to urge those around us to embrace authenticity. Recognizing and accepting our true selves is not only a spiritual mandate but a societal necessity, aptly echoed in William Shakespeare's "Hamlet". The timeless words, "This above all: to thine own self be true, and it must follow, as the night the day, thou canst not then be false to any man", resonate profoundly today, encouraging us to foster a community grounded in truth and sincerity.

The scriptures too, beckon us towards introspection and authenticity. In Luke 6:39-42, we are warned of the perils of hypocrisy, urging us to first address our flaws before pointing out others'.

> **39 He also told them a parable: "Can a blind person guide a blind person? Will not both fall into a pit? 40 A disciple is not above the teacher, but every disciple who is fully qualified will be like the teacher. 41 Why do you see the speck in your neighbor's eye but do not notice the log in your own eye? 42 Or how can you say to your neighbor, 'Friend, let me take out the speck in your eye,' when you yourself do not see the log in your own eye? You hypocrite, first take the log out of your own eye, and then you will see clearly to take the speck out of your neighbor's eye.**

This lesson is particularly relevant today, as the world grapples with the pandemic. It serves as a reminder to cultivate self-awareness and foster a society where individuals are encouraged to be forthright and genuine, thereby building a community resilient to the challenges we face.

As we stand at this critical juncture, let us commit to the following:

- **Be Authentic with Your Emotions** – Let our hearts reflect true feelings, fostering empathy and understanding in our communities.

- **Hold True to Your Beliefs** – Let our minds be grounds of honesty, promoting a society that respects and acknowledges diverse viewpoints.
- **Embrace Sincerity in Your Actions** – Let our attitudes mirror genuine intentions, building a world that thrives on trust and collaboration.

As we continue to wear our physical masks to protect one another, let us also take a moment to unmask the pretentiousness within, paving the way to a society that is free from the shackles of deceit and falsehood. Remember, it's time to Wear a Mask but Unmask Pretentiousness – and step into a world that embraces reality and freedom. Let's move forward, unmasked and free from shame.

Wear a mask if you must but unmask shamefulness. Be Free!

2. Shamefulness- Be free
(Embrace your authentic self)

Have you ever found yourself caught in the enthralling narrative of a movie or series, where the villain evokes such strong disdain that seeing the actor in real life triggers an automatic recoil? It's not uncommon to hear about actors receiving threats or facing public ridicule for portraying such characters, sometimes even grappling with shame themselves. This scenario, although extracted from fiction, mirrors a deep-rooted societal issue where individuals, driven by the fear of judgment and rejection, adorn various masks, desperately seeking applause and approval from others.

Many find themselves ensnared in a perpetual pursuit of human approval, defining their self-worth and dignity based on the perceptions and validations of others, rather than anchoring their identity in God's view of them. In this relentless chase, they often lose their true selves, conforming tirelessly to meet societal expectations, akin to actors on a stage, thriving on applause and laughter.

This grim reality brings to mind Jesus' cautionary advice to his disciples: "Take care not to perform righteous deeds in order that people may see them..." This timeless wisdom sheds light on the heart of hypocrisy that plagues many. The crippling fear of criticism and rejection, coupled with the relentless spotlight on our inadequacies, often catapults us into a vortex of shame and self-doubt.

However, it's vital to realize that our perceived flaws and past missteps are not beyond the reach of God's grace. A preacher wisely noted, "Your biggest sins are not too big for God's grace." As we navigate the intricate web of life, the desire to be loved, appreciated, and valued is innate. Yet, the true challenge lies in remaining authentic to God, oneself, and others amidst the mounting pressures of societal norms.

Brothers and sisters in faith, the journey towards self-love begins with embracing our imperfections, acknowledging that we are continuously evolving, a beautiful work in progress. To the brother, to the man of God, you have to love you. To the sister, woman of God, you have to love you. It requires shedding the numerous masks we wear to conceal our hurts and fears, fostering an environment of truth and trust. Remember, life may throw unforeseen challenges our way, but the power to respond with grace and authenticity remains within our grasp.

As we stand at the threshold of self-discovery, let us cherish the freedom to be ourselves, to choose authenticity over pretense, encouraging one another to discard the shackles of shame and to boldly step into the light of God's unconditional love and grace. It's time to unmask the shamefulness that confines us, ushering in an era where we can freely and fully be ourselves, anchored in God's profound love and acceptance.

Wearing A Mask But Unmasking Ungratefulness - Be Thankful!

3. Ungratefulness - Be Thankful

In times of difficulty and uncertainty, it is all too easy to focus on what we lack, rather than acknowledging the blessings that remain. It's vital, now more than ever, to cultivate a spirit of thankfulness. Webster's Dictionary describes "ingratitude" as the "forgetfulness of, or poor return for, kindness received." This ingratitude can often manifest as unexpressed gratitude, highlighting a fundamental lack of appreciation for our current blessings.

In this vein, let us heed the words of the Apostle Paul, who once warned Timothy of a society marred by selfishness and arrogance, where people would be "lovers of themselves, lovers of money, boasters, arrogant..." and above all, ungrateful (2 Timothy 3:1-4). These cautionary words echo loudly in our current times, urging us to introspect and realign our perspectives.

The eloquent preacher Dan Santiago helps us understand the roots of ingratitude, suggesting that:

> "We are too self-righteous- we think we deserve it. We are too forgetful- we don't realise that He did it. We are too discontented- it's never enough, always wanting more. It's too common, too free, too much. We never think it would come to an end or lose it."

Santiago encourages us to be "real with thankfulness," a call that resonates deeply in these turbulent times. Similarly, the Apostle Paul emphasized the virtue of contentment in his letter to the Philippians, highlighting the ability to find satisfaction in every circumstance through spiritual strength (Philippians 4:11-13).

> **11 Not that I am referring to being in need, for I have learned to be content with whatever I have. 12 I know what it is to have little, and I know what it is to have plenty. In any and all circumstances I have learned the secret of being well-fed and of going hungry, of having plenty and of being in need. 13 I can do all things through him who strengthens me.**

In practice, fostering thankfulness involves a conscious daily effort, recognizing the manifestations of God's faithfulness, sovereignty, and power in our lives. Whether facing health challenges, relationship strife, or other personal trials, we find solace and strength in giving thanks. As outlined in Psalms 103:2-5, **Bless the Lord, O my soul, and do not forget all his benefits—3 who forgives all your iniquity, who heals all your diseases, 4 who redeems your life from the Pit, who crowns you with steadfast love and mercy, 5 who satisfies you with good as long as you live[a]so that your youth is renewed like the eagle's.** We are reminded not to forget the countless benefits bestowed upon us, which renew and sustain us daily.

During the trying period of the Covid-19 pandemic, our resilience was tested in unprecedented ways. Despite the adversities, we were not severed from the avenues of prayer, praise, and promoting Christ's teachings. Even while physically distant, we were urged to maintain social connections, reminding each other of our collective responsibility and interconnectedness.

As we navigated the challenges brought on by the pandemic, wearing masks became a necessity, a symbol of protection and caution. Let us now translate this vigilance into unmasking pretentiousness and embracing authenticity in our lives. Let us replace shame with freedom, ingratitude with thankfulness. In counting our blessings, we will indeed find ourselves surprised by the magnitude of God's work in our lives.

Now, as we stand at the crossroads, let us resolve to emerge as better versions of ourselves, enriched by the lessons learned during the crisis. Our experiences have reaffirmed that in times of crisis, we are never truly isolated from God's grace and the support of our loved ones.

Let us pledge to foster a community grounded in love and compassion, aspiring to be better people for the Lord amidst and beyond the pandemic's confines.

A Call to
Trust God in
Difficult Times

WHEN IT'S ABOUT TO RUN OUT – HOPE

In moments of sheer despair and depletion, where do we find the sustenance to carry on? The scripture in 1 Kings 17:8-16 isn't just a story; it is a clarion call to embrace hope and trust in God's infinite providence during the most trying times. This narrative stands as a living testament, guiding us to navigate through life's adversities with unwavering faith and resilience.

1Kings 17:8-16

> ⁸ Then the word of the Lord came to him, saying, ⁹ "Go now to Zarephath, which belongs to Sidon, and live there; for I have commanded a widow there to feed you." ¹⁰ So he set out and went to Zarephath. When he came to the gate of the town, a widow was there gathering sticks; he called to her and said, "Bring me a little water in a vessel, so that I may drink." ¹¹ As she was going to bring it, he called to her and said, "Bring me a morsel of bread in your hand." ¹² But she said, "As the Lord

your God lives, I have nothing baked, only a handful of meal in a jar, and a little oil in a jug; I am now gathering a couple of sticks, so that I may go home and prepare it for myself and my son, that we may eat it, and die." [13] Elijah said to her, "Do not be afraid; go and do as you have said; but first make me a little cake of it and bring it to me, and afterwards make something for yourself and your son. [14] For thus says the Lord the God of Israel: The jar of meal will not be emptied and the jug of oil will not fail until the day that the Lord sends rain on the earth." [15] She went and did as Elijah said, so that she as well as he and her household ate for many days. [16] The jar of meal was not emptied, neither did the jug of oil fail, according to the word of the Lord that he spoke by Elijah.

This story occurs after the prophet Elijah stands before King Ahab and tells him there shall be no dew or rain these years except by my word. Then the word of God comes to the prophet, **"Go by the brook."** The ravens will feed him bread and meat in the morning and evening and he will drink water from the brook. After a while, the brook dries up and there is no rain.

For the widow that the prophet is sent to, things are running out, for she is:

Widowed – her husband, the one who would have provided shelter, food and protection is dead.

She has a son – those who have children would testify that they can eat you out of house and land. As most Caribbean islands adopted online classes for students (a hybrid model) and children were at home, they ate more.

There is a drought –no water, no rain, wells have dried up, no drinking water, animals struggling, plants and trees not producing properly. Much like what we in Barbados have experienced during our dry season, which runs from January to June.

Along comes this prophet of God with demands.

Demands of others.

It is one thing to be dealing with your own issues, but when others make demands of you and you have dependents, that's added stress, added pressure, and this often leads people to their tipping or breaking point.

When we are about to run out or have come to the end of ourselves, we can – hope in the providence of God.

1. Hope In The Providence of God

> , ⁹ **"Go now to Zarephath, which belongs to Sidon, and live there; for I have commanded a widow there to feed you."**
> ¹⁰ **So he set out and went to Zarephath.**

"The word "providence" comes from the Latin *providentia* (Gk. *Pronoia* [provnoia]) and means foresight or making provision beforehand. Providence, then, is the sovereign, divine superintendence of all things."² It is hope in the God who has already provided.

Hope in God's Omnipotence.

The word omnipotent comes from two Latin words *that when translated means* "all power." We are hoping in the God who has all the power. Nothing is therefore too hard, too difficult or impossible for Him to do. As depicted in the story, God's power knows no bounds, orchestrating miraculous provisions even in the direst circumstances. The songs of faith express Him as a God who is bigger than our mountains and will do exceeding, abundantly above all we can ask, think or imagine. To deepen our trust, we can meditate on the teachings of Matthew 6:25-34, finding assurance that our needs will not go unnoticed in God's watchful eyes.

> [25] **"Therefore I tell you, do not worry about your life, what you will eat or what you will drink,[a] or about your body, what you will wear. Is not life more than food and the body more than clothing?** [26] **Look at the birds of the air: they neither sow nor reap nor gather into barns, and yet your heavenly Father feeds them. Are you not of more value than they?** [27] **And which of you by worrying can add a single hour to your span of life?[b]** [28] **And why do you worry about clothing? Consider the lilies of the field, how they grow; they neither toil nor spin,** [29] **yet I tell you, even Solomon in all his glory was not clothed like one of these.** [30] **But if God so clothes the grass of the field, which is alive today and tomorrow is thrown into the oven, will he not much more clothe you—you**

of little faith? ³¹ **Therefore do not worry, saying, 'What will we eat?' or 'What will we drink?' or 'What will we wear?' ³² For it is the gentiles who seek all these things, and indeed your heavenly Father knows that you need all these things. ³³ But seek first the kingdom of God[c] and his[d] righteousness, and all these things will be given to you as well.**

³⁴ **"So do not worry about tomorrow, for tomorrow will bring worries of its own. Today's trouble is enough for today.**

Hope in the providence of God is hope in *God's omnipresence.*

Omnipresence is derived from two Latin words that when translated mean "all- present". God's omnipresence, illustrated vividly in Elijah's story, assures us that we are never alone in our struggles. God is here, there, anywhere and everywhere. He is close to everyone, next to everyone. He is not limited by geography, time or space. The comfort this brings is that God is with us. The further assurance is that even though God is with me, His being with me does not stop Him from being with you also. In other words, you are not alone. Yes, there are times we may feel like we are all by ourselves. We feel that the decisions are ours to make. But even in those moments, God is with us. God is with you.

Hope in the providence of God is hope in *God's omniscience.*

By now you have probably figured out that this as well comes from two Latin words that when translated means, "all-knowledge." God is all knowing. He knows everything that is knowable or that can be known. He knows the past, the present and the future. We can trust God and entrust ourselves to Him because He knows the future and nothing takes Him by surprise.

Hope in the providence of God is hope in **God's Omnibenevolence.**

This one I recently discovered, as it was always the above three when talking about the Omnis' of God. God is omnibenevolent as He is all-loving, or infinitely good. We often say as Moravians, **"God is good all the time and all the time God is good."** Since God is perfect, being perfectly good must entail being good in all ways at all times and towards all other beings.

When it's about to run out, hope in the providence of God, but also hope in the process of God.

Drawing inspiration from the narrative, we are encouraged to foster a hopeful outlook, firmly rooted in the belief of God's loving and timely provisions. It calls us to transcend our fears and anxieties, fostering a spirit that remains buoyant, optimistic, and firmly grounded in God's promises.

2. Hope In The Process of God

Scriptures often narrate processes that defy human logic yet are divinely orchestrated to foster profound faith. Take, for instance, Naaman's directive in 2 Kings 5 to wash in the Jordan River seven times for healing, or Jesus healing the blind man in an unorthodox manner as described in John 9. These processes, though seemingly irrational, were means to cultivate a deeper faith in God's wisdom and plans.

In our personal journeys, we might encounter processes orchestrated by God to deepen our faith, akin to the trials faced by the children of Israel in their wilderness journey. We might feel the urge to abort this process when the pressure mounts, forgetting that these are the very circumstances that forge our faith, akin to the pressure that creates diamonds, the fire that refines gold or the agitation that births pearls.

Therefore, in times of trials, let us lean not on our understanding but adhere faithfully to God's instructions, as outlined in Romans 8 and Proverbs 3:5-7. For, in following God's process, even when it seems inexplicable, we find the true essence of hope and divine provision.

When it's about to run out- Hope in the provision of God.

3. Hope In The Provision of God- Jehovah Jireh

In moments where resources seem scant and despair looms large, remember Elijah's prophecy - a promise of unending provision during the drought (1 Kings 17:14-16).

> **[14] For thus says the Lord the God of Israel: The jar of meal will not be emptied and the jug of oil will not fail until the day that the Lord sends rain on the earth." [15] She went and did as Elijah said, so that she as well as he and her household ate for many days. [16] The jar of meal was not emptied, neither did the jug of oil fail, according to the word of the Lord that he spoke by Elijah.**

Talk about a miracle of provision! Look at God's timing! As you read, be reminded that the promises of God are sure: "Yes" and "Amen." God is not like man that God should lie. He will supply and provide all of your needs according to His riches in glory. Faith is needed as we allow God to process us, refine us, to agitate us. Process often leads to a refining of our hearts to have compassion, for us to have better character, for us to learn more and grow closer to HIM, and moreover closer to who He has called us to be this side of Heaven. God meets us at our point of need, providing not just for our physical needs but refining our character and drawing us closer to Him.

I recall a time of personal refinement during my preparation to become a minister of the gospel. I was leaving family, work and everything I knew and love, to go to Jamaica (which I love). But there were so many horror stories being told back in 1998 that, I was also afraid. There was the cultural adjustment and then academics and ministry formation. The student's association, however had a slogan: 'There are stages and stages and still more stages.' This helped me to keep trusting God, to trust God's process when I doubted the call and doubted myself. I trusted Him when courses and assignments were difficult. In failing you feel like a failure. Still, that's not the time to abandon the process.

Even though the process may feel or is actually hard or sometimes overwhelming, it will work for our good. Faith is required in the journey, and we must never forget to praise God and ask Him to show us the journey. We must ask Him to clear paths for us and help us to be bold through the process.

Journeys also keep us close to our Father — the One who is the finisher of our faith. We must remember that we are not the finishers of our own faith.

The Psalmist David would have testified of that. **He states in Psalm 23:1 "The Lord is my Shepherd. I shall not want."**

You shall not want either.

Watch this: God took the widow from one (1) last meal: a

little flour, and a little oil. She, the prophet and her household ate for many days. We are reminded here again, that faith is a journey.

I pray that even now, as you read this chapter, may the Sovereign God who, is our Jehovah Jireh, multiply, stretch and increase you. I pray that:

God will stretch your money.
God will stretch your salary.
God will stretch your food.
God will stretch the gas in your car.
God will cause the water leak not to get worse till a time.

He is able. God is able. He provides grace.
The Word of God cannot fail. The Word of God will not fail!
There is a song we sing. It goes like this: "***There is nothing that I need that He won't supply. There is nothing that I need that He won't provide. If I believe, Lord, I believe. I will say to the mountain move, I will say to the mountain get out of my way.***"
What is running out, declare that it will run over!
Hope in the Lord. Since I believe that life and death are in the power of the tongue, I just want to speak over your life and situation. I pray that God will provide and that He supplies your needs in the name of Jesus – with miracles, signs and wonders following.

As you navigate through challenging seasons, may you experience Jehovah Jireh in your life - a God who stretches your resources, who provides exceedingly and abundantly, meeting every need according to His riches in glory. May this chapter serve as a reminder to place your trust in God's provisions, even when it seems like resources are running out.

Embrace the journey with God, anchor your hope in the Lord, in His providence, in His process, and in His provision. Let the testimonies in this chapter inspire you to declare that what seems to be running out will soon be running over, fostering an everlasting hope in the Lord.

WHEN WE LOSE EVERYTHING – FAITH

In moments where darkness seems to engulf every ounce of our joy, where trials seem relentless, and hope appears to be a distant memory, the tale of Job serves as a beacon of light, a testament to unwavering faith in the face of unimaginable suffering.

Job 1:13-22

One day when his sons and daughters were eating and drinking wine in the eldest brother's house, ¹⁴ a messenger came to Job and said, "The oxen were plowing and the donkeys were feeding beside them, ¹⁵ and the Sabeans fell on them and carried them off, and killed the servants with the edge of the sword; I alone have escaped to tell you." ¹⁶ While he was still speaking, another came and said, "The fire of God fell from heaven and burned up the sheep and the servants, and consumed them; I alone have escaped to tell you." ¹⁷ While he

**was still speaking, another came and said,
"The Chaldeans formed three columns,
made a raid on the camels and carried
them off, and killed the servants with the
edge of the sword; I alone have escaped
to tell you."** [18] **While he was still speaking,
another came and said, "Your sons and
daughters were eating and drinking
wine in their eldest brother's house,** [19]
**and suddenly a great wind came across
the desert, struck the four corners of the
house, and it fell on the young people,
and they are dead; I alone have escaped
to tell you."**

[20] **Then Job arose, tore his robe, shaved
his head, and fell on the ground and
worshiped.** [21] **He said, "Naked I came
from my mother's womb, and naked shall
I return there; the Lord gave, and the Lord
has taken away; blessed be the name of
the Lord."**

[22] **In all this Job did not sin or charge God
with wrongdoing.**

We, in this era, unfortunately have a brand of Christianity
that believes we are too blessed and anointed for anything bad
to happen to us. This version of Christian thought and living
has created a "disconnect" and "crisis" for those who are not
grounded in the totality of the Bible – both the Old and New
Testament. In fact, the Bible and Christianity are two of the
few belief systems and works of miracles known across the

world which, have stood the test of time and space, and which actually confirms, **"I have told you all this so that you may have peace in me. Here on earth you will have many trials and sorrows. But take heart, because I have overcome the world." John 16:33 NLT**

It is therefore even more helpful to consider what happened to one of the most blameless, righteous men who feared God and turned away from evil. What happened to the Biblical character Job? Job experienced loss. What did Job lose?

He lost his wealth.

> **"The oxen were plowing and the donkeys were feeding beside them, ¹⁵ and the Sabeans fell on them and carried them off, and killed the servants with the edge of the sword; I alone have escaped to tell you." ¹⁶ While he was still speaking, another came and said, "The fire of God fell from heaven and burned up the sheep and the servants, and consumed them; I alone have escaped to tell you." ¹⁷ While he was still speaking, another came and said, "The Chaldeans formed three columns, made a raid on the camels and carried them off, and killed the servants with the edge of the sword; I alone have escaped to tell you."**

He lost his family

> **18 While he was still speaking, another came and said, "Your sons and daughters were eating and drinking wine in their eldest brother's house, 19 and suddenly a great wind came across the desert, struck the four corners of the house, and it fell on the young people, and they are dead; I alone have escaped to tell you."**

Think about this for a moment. Let this sink into your spirit. Seven sons, three daughters- all of his children – from the eldest, who was next in line, to the youngest. The future of the family name, the family lineage – all gone.

I dare say that **Job also lost his wife.**

Lost can bring deep hurt. Alright! I know, the Bible does not say that he divorced her or she divorced him, but her words are words of one not prepared to stay with, or journey with Job during this catastrophic time. Could it be that these words reflect her lack of support to keep trusting in God?

> **9 Then his wife said to him, "Do you still persist in your integrity? Curse[j] God and die." 10 But he said to her, "You speak as any foolish woman would speak. Shall we receive good from God and not receive evil?" In all this Job did not sin with his lips.**

I further submit to you that Job was about to **lose his legacy.**

"There was once a man in the land of
Uz whose name was Job. That man was
blameless and upright, one who feared
God and turned away from evil. So that
this man was the greatest of all the people
of the east. ⁴ His sons used to go and hold
feasts in one another's houses in turn; and
they would send and invite their three
sisters to eat and drink with them. ⁵ And
when the feast days had run their course,
Job would send and sanctify them, and he
would rise early in the morning and offer
burnt offerings according to the number
of them all; for Job said, "It may be that
my children have sinned, and cursed God
in their hearts."

This is what Job always did.

Will all of this stop now that his life has been impacted,
affected, decimated? Do we only worship and serve God
because good things are happening to us? It is so interesting
that Satan is of the belief that God's creation only serves Him
because of the good that he experiences

.⁹ Then Satan[f] answered the Lord, "Does
Job fear God for nothing? ¹⁰ Have you not
put a fence around him and his house and
all that he has, on every side? You have
blessed the work of his hands, and his
possessions have increased in the land. ¹¹
But stretch out your hand now, and touch
all that he has, and he will curse you to
your face."

Therefore, I encourage you that when you lose everything, have faith that stands in the sufferings of life. Honestly, God uses the decimation of our lives to bring full and true worship to Him from His children, as His children are foremost made for worship beyond their needs and wants.

1. Faith That Stands In The Sufferings Of Life.

As we suffer and go through the losses of job, family, friends and normalcy of life, we must keep believing in our God to be with us and to guide us through each step of the way. Hebrews 11:1 (NIV) reverberates the essence of faith, stating, "Now faith is confidence in what we hope for and assurance about what we do not see."

No matter which translation you may read it from, and here are a few, these are powerful words.

> **New Revised Standard Version (NRSV) states, "Faith is the <u>assurance</u> of things hoped for, the conviction of things not seen."**

> **New Living Translation (NLT) says, "Faith <u>shows</u> the reality of what we hope for; it is the evidence of things we cannot see."**

> **English Standard Version (ESV) says" "Now faith is the <u>assurance </u>of things hoped for, the conviction of things not seen."**

This scripture encapsulates the spiritual fortitude and resilience that characterized Job's journey. Faith, therefore, manifests as an unyielding belief in God's divine purpose, even when the path seems unclear and fraught with obstacles. It is a confidence, a conviction in God's character and as such, God's ability. It is the belief in the greatness and goodness of God. I, however, caution that things more often than not get worse before they often get better.

Job Loses His Health

"And Satan[b] also came among them to present himself before the Lord. 2 The Lord said to Satan, [c] "Where have you come from?" Satan[d] answered the Lord, "From going to and fro on the earth, and from walking up and down on it." 3 The Lord said to Satan, [e] "Have you considered my servant Job? There is no one like him on the earth, a blameless and upright man who fears God and turns away from evil. He still persists in his integrity, although you incited me against him, to destroy him for no reason." 4 Then Satan[f] answered the Lord, "Skin for skin! All that people have they will give to save their lives. [g] 5 But stretch out your hand now and touch his bone and his flesh, and he will curse you to your face." 6 The Lord said to Satan, [h] "Very well, he is in your power; only spare his life."

7 So Satan[i] went out from the presence of the Lord, and inflicted loathsome sores on Job from the sole of his foot to the crown of his head. 8 Job[j] took a potsherd with which to scrape himself, and sat among the ashes.

The narrative of Job plunges us into the depths of human suffering. It is easy to sing when the sun is shining and you are in the sanctuary. But can you sing when you are in hospital, when you have been turned down for the job, the loan, the partnership, or something as simple as losing a friend, or as earth shattering as losing a parent or a spouse? **Sometimes it gets worse before it gets better.** Watch how bad it got. In Job Chapter 2:11-13, take note of verse 12.

[11] Now when Job's three friends heard of all these troubles that had come upon him, each of them set out from his home— Eliphaz the Temanite, Bildad the Shuhite, and Zophar the Naamathite. They met together to go and console and comfort him. [12] When they saw him from a distance, they did not recognize him, and they raised their voices and wept aloud; they tore their robes and threw dust in the air upon their heads. [13] They sat with him on the ground seven days and seven nights, and no one spoke a word to him, for they saw that his suffering was very great."

Job's friends did not recognise him, and no one said anything for seven days and nights because the suffering was great. Truth is, sometimes we don't know what to say. The calamities that befall some people, some islands and countries leave us speechless. But have faith in God through the sufferings of life. God never promised us a life without suffering. In fact, God promises trouble, but we are to take heart as He also promises that He has control over this world. You do not only suffer because you have committed some sin or because you are poor or because somebody is out to get you and is working something on you. Sometimes, we suffer because we are called.

We encounter our own "Jobs' moments." These could range from grappling with the loss of a loved one, battling illness, or facing financial instability. Yet, within these trials lies an opportunity: to forge an unbreakable bond with God, to find solace and guidance in our faith.

Strength emerges from testing. The products we use, the cars we drive, chairs we sit in- are tested to see if they can hold up under all the possible conditions the users would put them through. Remember the three Hebrew boys whom thrown into a fiery furnace in the Book of Daniel? Remember the apostles before the council? They were flogged and told not to speak the name of Jesus. As they suffered, they kept their faith in God. I encourage you to do the same.

It is important to acknowledge that the journey isn't devoid of doubts and moments of weakness. Job's transformation wasn't instantaneous. It was a gradual process, characterized by questioning, despair, and eventually, profound enlightenment. Similarly, our faith journeys are marred by moments of vulnerability. Yet, it is in these moments that our faith can truly flourish, as we learn to lean on God's eternal wisdom and grace.

As these scriptures encouraged me may they also encourage you.

> [10] And after you have suffered for a little while, the God of all grace, who has called you to his eternal glory in Christ, will himself restore, support, strengthen, and establish you. 1 Peter 5:10

> And not only that, but we[a] also boast in our sufferings, knowing that suffering produces endurance, [4] and endurance produces character, and character produces hope, [5] and hope does not disappoint us, because God's love has been poured into our hearts through the Holy Spirit that has been given to us. Romans 5:3-5

The above is critical to Christian thought and to Christian life. Growth is part of God's purpose for us.

> [18] I consider that the sufferings of this present time are not worth comparing with the glory about to be revealed to us... [24] For in[a] hope we were saved. Now hope that is seen is not hope. For who hopes[b] for what is seen? [25] But if we hope for what we do not see, we wait for it with patience. Romans 8:18, 24-25

> [6] In this you rejoice,[a] even if now for a little while you have had to suffer various trials, [7] so that the genuineness of your faith—being more precious than gold that, though perishable, is tested by fire—may be found to result in praise and glory and honour

when Jesus Christ is revealed. [8] **Although
you have not seen[b] Him, you love Him;
and even though you do not see Him now,
you believe in Him and rejoice with an
indescribable and glorious joy,** [9] **for you are
receiving the outcome of your faith, the
salvation of your souls. 1 Peter 1:6-9.**

2. Faith That Stands In The Sovereignty of God

In the intricate tapestry of life's trials and tribulations, we
find solace in understanding the grandeur narrative unfolding
behind the scenes. This greater picture is vividly illustrated in
the discourse between God and Satan, revealing an essence of
faith anchored in God's sovereignty:

Job 1

[6] **One day the heavenly beings[a] came to
present themselves before the Lord, and
Satan[b] also came among them.** [7] **The
Lord said to Satan,[c] "Where have you
come from?" Satan[d] answered the Lord,
"From going to and fro on the earth,
and from walking up and down on it."**
[8] **The Lord said to Satan,[e] "Have you
considered my servant Job? There is no
one like him on the earth, a blameless
and upright man who fears God and turns
away from evil."** [9] **Then Satan[f] answered
the Lord, "Does Job fear God for nothing?**
[10] **Have you not put a fence around him**

and his house and all that he has, on every side? You have blessed the work of his hands, and his possessions have increased in the land. [11] But stretch out your hand now, and touch all that he has, and he will curse you to your face." [12] The Lord said to Satan,[g] "Very well, all that he has is in your power; only do not stretch out your hand against him!" So Satan[h] went out from the presence of the Lord.

Job 2

One day the heavenly beings[a] came to present themselves before the Lord, and Satan[b] also came among them to present himself before the Lord. [2] The Lord said to Satan,[c] "Where have you come from?" Satan[d] answered the Lord, "From going to and fro on the earth, and from walking up and down on it." [3] The Lord said to Satan,[e] "Have you considered my servant Job? There is no one like him on the earth, a blameless and upright man who fears God and turns away from evil. He still persists in his integrity, although you incited me against him, to destroy him for no reason." [4] Then Satan[f] answered the Lord, "Skin for skin! All that people have they will give to save their lives.[g] [5] But stretch out your hand now and touch his bone and his flesh, and he will curse you to your face." ⁶ The Lord said to Satan,[h] "Very well, he is in your power; only spare his life."

⁷ So Satan[i] went out from the presence of the Lord, and inflicted loathsome sores on Job from the sole of his foot to the crown of his head. ⁸ Job[j] took a potsherd with which to scrape himself, and sat among the ashes.

This profound revelation illuminates the notion that our sufferings are not mere arbitrary events but can be perceived as divine tests orchestrated to refine our faith and spiritual fortitude. Through this lens, we are encouraged to nurture a faith founded on the understanding of a God who:

God who choses me – Have you considered my servant Job? That's the question God puts to Satan. It was God's idea. Job was God's choice for the test. Just as Job was chosen, we too are selected to withstand and prevail in our respective trials.

God who has confidence in me – There is no one like him in all the earth, a blameless and upright man who fears God and turns away from evil. That was God's view/thought/ belief about Job.

The second time around God adds this part- **"He still persists in his integrity, although you incited me against him, to destroy him for no reason."**

God has confidence in us to make the right choice, to do His will, to trust and serve Him even in difficult times. He has confidence in our ability to choose righteousness, even amidst adversity. This trust, consequently, births blessings and spiritual growth, fostering a symbiotic relationship of faith and grace between us and God.

Remember, before we discuss, what faith is: **"Now faith is confidence in what we hope for and assurance about what we do not see."**

We as believers, saints, ambassadors for Christ, must, under the specific challenges we face, understand that those difficulties are handpicked for us by God. God considered Job. He considered you, and He will restore you and bless you, as you and I grow in our faith and in confidence in Him. The tests are often there to show us who we are and where we need to grow. They show us what we believe in our hearts to be true.

Think about this even more:

> **God who has compassion and mercy –**
> **[6]"The Lord said to Satan,[h] "Very well, he**
> **is in your power; only spare his life."**

Despite the severity of our trials, God's compassion remains a constant pillar of support. This is evident from His instruction to Satan to spare Job's life, reflecting His boundless grace and concern for us. How would Job have known that God told Satan to spare his life? And yet that is the nature of the God we serve; to grant grace and mercy to us. These truths resound in the powerful words of John 3:16-17:

> [16] **"For God so loved the world that He gave His only Son, so that everyone who believes in Him may not perish but have eternal life.[17] "Indeed, God did not send the Son into the world to condemn the world, but in order that the world might be saved through Him.**

God's enduring love manifests in His persistent desire to

save and sustain us, affirming that we are never forsaken, even in the eye of the storm. Thus, we embrace a faith that is deeply rooted in God's character – a God who has chosen us, believes in us, and extends unyielding compassion towards us. Just like Job, who professed in **Job 23:8-11**

> "If I go forward, He is not there; or backward, I cannot perceive Him; [9] on the left He hides, and I cannot behold Him; I turn[c] to the right, but I cannot see Him. [10] But He knows the way that I take; when He has tested me, I shall come out like gold. [11] My foot has held fast to His steps; I have kept His way and have not turned aside.

We too can cultivate a confidence that, through God's grace, our trials will mold us into beings of refined gold, unwavering in our faith and resolute in our spiritual journey. By fostering this kind of faith, we not only endure the challenges appointed to us but also grow exponentially in our spiritual walk, buoyed by a God who loves, guides, and nurtures us unconditionally.

3. Faith That Stands In The Strength of God

> [20] Then Job arose, tore his robe, shaved his head, and fell on the ground and worshiped. 21 He said, "Naked I came from my mother's womb, and naked shall I return there; the Lord gave, and the Lord has taken away; blessed be the name of

the Lord." 22 In all this Job did not sin or charge God with wrongdoing.

In the face of profound sorrow and loss, we witness Job embodying a faith that transcends human understanding—a faith firmly anchored in the might of God. This remarkable testament of faith impels us to be stalwart worshipers, persisting even as we navigate through life's most harrowing storms: be it illness, loss, heartache, or unprecedented global crises. It beckons us to emulate Job's undying spirit of worship, fueled not by our human resilience but by a supernatural strength derived from an unwavering faith in God. As the scriptures affirm, Job remained steadfast, refraining from attributing any wrong to God amidst his trials. Verse 22 tells us: **"For in all this Job did not sin or charge God with wrongdoing."**

Reflect further on Job's fervent proclamation in Job 19:

> **"O that my words were written down! O that they were inscribed in a book!**[24] **O that with an iron pen and with lead they were engraved on a rock forever!**[25] **For I know that my Redeemer**[b] **lives, and that at the last he**[c] **will stand upon the earth;**[d][26] **and after my skin has been thus destroyed, then in**[e] **my flesh I shall see God,**[f][27] **whom I shall see on my side,**[g] **and my eyes shall behold, and not another. My heart faints within me!**

Inspired by such unyielding faith, various artistes have expressed this sentiment through music that reverberates with hope and resilience. Songs like Tremaine Hawkins' where the lyrics echo:

"I never lost my hope, I never lost my joy, I never lost my faith, But most of all, I never lost my praise."

And in the vibrant rhythms of Katalys Crew which resound with the bold declaration:

"You can take away my home, take away my car, You can never take my faith in the Lord. You can take away my life, whatever it may be, but You cannot take my Lord."

These words encapsulate a faith that is all-encompassing, resilient, and apt for every season of our lives. This is a faith more versatile and adaptive than any tool or substance known to man, for it is grounded in the living God. In your journey, may you grasp this profound truth—that no challenge is insurmountable when you stand hand in hand with God. Embrace the certainty that if God guided you to a situation, He will surely see you through it.

Therefore, stand unflinching, without yielding to despair or disbelief. Don't give up. Don't give in. Don't stop believing. Even when stripped of all worldly possessions and comforts, hold firm to a faith that perseveres through life's sufferings—a faith sustained by the sovereign God who handpicks us, nurtures us with compassion, believes in our potential, and showers us with undying concern. Let your faith be an unbreakable fortress, fortified in the immense strength of God.

WHEN THINGS WON'T CHANGE – HAVE DETERMINATION

Mark 5: 25-34

25 Now there was a woman who had been suffering from a flow of blood for twelve years. 26 She had endured much under many physicians and had spent all that she had, and she was no better but rather grew worse. 27 She had heard about Jesus and came up behind him in the crowd and touched his cloak, 28 for she said, "If I but touch his cloak, I will be made well." 29 Immediately her flow of blood stopped, and she felt in her body that she was healed of her disease. 30 Immediately aware that power had gone forth from him, Jesus turned about in the crowd and said, "Who touched my cloak?" 31 And his disciples said to him, "You see the crowd pressing in on you; how can you say, 'Who touched me?'" 32 He looked all around to see who

**had done it. ³³ But the woman, knowing
what had happened to her, came in fear
and trembling, fell down before him, and
told him the whole truth. ³⁴ He said to her,
"Daughter, your faith has made you well;
go in peace, and be healed of your disease."**

In a world that is ever-evolving, it might appear paradoxical
to consider the aspects that seem immutable, that resist change
despite our fervent efforts. What do you do, when no matter
what you do, who you go to, or when you do it- it's the same
end result? I did a Bible study series recently, titled, "Lord Help
Me To Forgive" and I fell in love again with The Serenity
Prayer. A mantra that helps us navigate the complex dichotomy
of changeability and unchangeability in our lives:

The Serenity Prayer

God, grant me the serenity
to accept the things I cannot change,
the courage to change the things I can,
and the wisdom to know the difference.
Living one day at a time;
enjoying one moment at a time;
accepting hardship as a pathway to peace;
taking, as Jesus did, this sinful world as it is.
Not as I would have it;
trusting that You will make all things right
if I surrender to Your will;
so that I may be reasonably happy in this life
and supremely happy with You forever in the next.

Amen.   Reinhold Niebuhr (1892-1971)³

There are some things we cannot change. Some scholars suggest that the fifth chapter of Mark offers us a glimpse into those realities that for the ancient world were not that easily changeable, that seemed insurmountable- a man possessed by a demon name Legion, living among tombs, a man who could not be restrained. A sick, dying girl who, eventually dies as Jesus stops to help the woman in our story.

We are never told her name. All we are told of is her condition. Often, society tends to define us by our hardships and past, a phenomenon as true today as it was during biblical times. What was her condition? Matthew Chapter 9:20–22, Mark Chapter 5:25–34, and Luke Chapter 8:43–48 all describe her as:

A woman suffering from a medical condition for 12 years.

Not for a week, or months, but 12 years.

A woman enduring much from people for 12 years. Luke's Gospel says, **"No one could cure her."**

A woman who spent much over the 12 years. In fact, she spent all she had on physicians.

A woman who was no better after 12 years but was worse. She was financially worse, physically worse and no doubt mentally worse.

So, the medication is not working, the behaviour of children and the spouse is not changing. Work is still the same. Pastor doesn't talk about the finances. Some say they are poor, peaceful and polite, or that they are too broke to even pay attention. Some people still don't like you. They won't talk to you, and COVID-19 is still around. Things are not changing. The frustration of stagnation can sometimes feel overwhelming, engulfing us in a cycle of despair and hopelessness.

You need determination. Some tell you to pre-determine in

your heart and mind. It is a mind-set prior to a task. Determination involves careful consideration of the requirements of a task and a decision that the task is worth whatever cost, expenses, and sacrifices necessary to achieve it. Despite the setbacks, we will forge ahead with renewed vigor. This form of determination is not just a mindset, but a profound commitment to oneself, a commitment to persist even when the circumstances seem bleak.

There are some things I can change, therefore when things won't change I have a determination to connect with Jesus.

1. Determination To Connect With Jesus

²⁷ She had heard about Jesus, and came up behind Him in the crowd and touched His cloak, ²⁸ for she said, "If I but touch His clothes, I will be made well."

After you have suffered, after you have endured, after you have spent, squandered, wasted; after things are not getting any better, why don't you connect with Jesus?

You have tried and tested many things, gotten many second and third opinions, but now might be the best season to seek God, to forge or rekindle a bond with Him. This is the time to move towards God, to recommit to God; to connect with God more consistently, more deeply in prayer, in reading the Word of God, and allowing the Holy Spirit to lead.

If anybody can help me; if anybody can help you, it's Jesus!

The term "touched" from the scripture connotes a deliberate grasp, a gesture borne out of a staunch determination, not a mere passing brush. This determined grasp instigated a life-altering transformation, as seen in verse 29:

Immediately her flow of blood stopped, and she felt in her body that she was healed of her disease.

When things won't change, have the determination to connect with Jesus. A connection that harbors the potential to induce a profound metamorphosis within you and your circumstances.

2. Determination To Come Out And Come Forward.

. [27] She had heard about Jesus, and came up behind Him in the crowd and touched His cloak, [28] for she said, "If I but touch His clothes, I will be made well."

Desperation often sparks audacious actions. We know that desperate people do desperate things. It prompts the fundamental questions: How fervently do you crave a change? What lengths are you willing to traverse to attain it? How committed are you to achieve it? Desperate circumstances beckon bold gestures. This woman exhibited an unyielding resolve amidst her challenges:

This woman was determined because in her condition:

She would have been physically weak (bleeding, losing blood constantly, day in and day out).

Sometimes you have to push yourself. With her continuous ailment, every step was an act of resilience. Sometimes, breaking through means stepping out of known territories, stepping out of your comfort zone, venturing beyond ingrained beliefs, attitudes, and behaviours.

She would have been socially unclean. The norms of her time, as documented in Leviticus 15:25-27, labelled her as impure, excluding her from social and religious spheres. Yet, her hunger for healing propelled her forward. How much of you have felt like outsiders, or the black sheep; the one not welcomed to the group?

The journey towards healing often entails confronting various obstacles and silencing self-doubt. It demands a courageous step forward, not only to forge a connection with Jesus but towards your blessings, seeking transformation and healing even when faced with discomfort and unease.

3. Determination To Change You- Peace

> ³⁰ Immediately aware that power had gone forth from him, Jesus turned about in the crowd and said, "Who touched my cloak?" ³¹ And his disciples said to him, "You see the crowd pressing in on you; how can you say, 'Who touched me?'" ³² He looked all around to see who had done it. ³³ But the woman, knowing what had happened to her, came in fear and trembling, fell down before him, and told him the whole truth. ³⁴ He said to her, "Daughter, your faith has made you well; go in peace, and be healed of your disease."

In life, we frequently encounter moments of weakness and discouragement where the weight of our burdens seems unbearable. It's in these moments where we find the true essence of change – a change catalyzed by an unwavering faith in God. My friend Serene once tearfully confessed, "It's painful feeling trapped with no way out. It's hard admitting to six suicide attempts, but I refuse to return to that darkness."

What is the "there" you are desperately striving to leave behind, to transform? It's time to alter our mindset, to confide wholeheartedly in God just like the woman who touched Jesus' garment, a sanctuary of understanding and compassion where no judgment resides.

Initiate a lifestyle revolution:

The Scriptures say, **"She told Him the whole truth."** Speak truth and be honest with God. She had to view Him as more than just another physician in Galilee or from Nazareth because she had tried many of them. Jesus became the confidant in whom she could bare her soul, and not feel judged or condemned. When you know what has happened to you and where you have come from and what you have been through, you are at peace speaking the truth and being you.

Change behaviour- live truth! Adjust your behaviour to embody integrity and authenticity.

Change lifestyle and receive the truth! Embrace and cherish truth.

Change to righteous. Live right and do right by others.

In my teachings on stewardship, I often remind students that there are four dimensions of our stewardship relationship. We must do right by God, do right to ourselves, do right to each other, and do right to God's creation.

Embody the change you aspire to see, fostering a life that glorifies God through persistent efforts of courage, consistency and commitment even amidst storms. Sometimes God stills the storm and sometimes He stills you in the storm. He gives you peace.

Through your unchanging season, keep holding on to God. Be encouraged by the chorus: ***"I am determined to hold on to the end. Jesus is with me, on Him I can depend for I know I*** *have salvation, I feel it in my soul. I am determined to hold on to the end."*

Hang on. Press on. Press through. Fight on, child of God, man of God, woman of God. The victory is ours in the name of Jesus.

When things won't change, have a determination to connect with Jesus, to come out and come forward and to change you. So sometimes our belief, our determination, our confidence in Christ must be stronger than what we feel or what we may want at any specific time.

As a teenager, I battled persistent scalp issues, a struggle that seemed unyielding despite numerous attempts at resolution. I insisted that the barber who, was generally a clean barber, sanitize the machine. It did not stop the bumps. Needless to say, I changed barbers. That also did not stop them from appearing. I tried all the creams, soaps and concoctions that could be recommended. Nothing changed. I have been to dermatologists in Barbados and the Caribbean, and still no change.

It was during a transformative journey to Egypt and Israel in 2008 that I experienced a profound change. As I immersed myself in the Dead Sea, despite the physical discomfort, I realized a shift within me, an awakening to the grace that God bestows upon us, enabling us to view our challenges through a lens of faith and resilience.

Sometimes, our battles remain unchanged, but what truly transforms is our perspective, our approach, and our reactions to them, guided by the divine grace that equips us with the strength to endure and thrive. Remember, in the face of complexities, pain, and frustrations, there lies an abundant reservoir of grace and fortitude from God awaiting to be tapped.

In moments of stagnancy, harbor a relentless determination

to connect with Jesus, to emerge and progress, and to foster a change within yourself. Recognize that sometimes our belief and conviction in Christ should surpass our current feelings or desires, paving the way for a resilient, faith-fortified journey towards healing and peace.

WHEN IT GETS TOO MUCH – PRAY!

Matthew 26:36-46

³⁶ Then Jesus went with them to a place called Gethsemane; and He said to His disciples, "Sit here while I go over there and pray." ³⁷ He took with Him Peter and the two sons of Zebedee, and began to be grieved and agitated. ³⁸ Then He said to them, "I am deeply grieved, even to death; remain here, and stay awake with Me." ³⁹ And going a little farther, He threw himself on the ground and prayed, "My Father, if it is possible, let this cup pass from me; yet not what I want but what you want." ⁴⁰ Then He came to the disciples and found them sleeping; and He said to Peter, "So, could you not stay awake with me one hour? ⁴¹ Stay awake and pray that you may not come into the time of trial;[a] the spirit indeed is willing, but the flesh is weak." ⁴² Again He went away for the second time and prayed, "My

Father, if this cannot pass unless I drink it, your will be done." [43] Again He came and found them sleeping, for their eyes were heavy. [44] So leaving them again, He went away and prayed for the third time, saying the same words. [45] Then He came to the disciples and said to them, "Are you still sleeping and taking your rest? See, the hour is at hand, and the Son of Man is betrayed into the hands of sinners. [46] Get up, let us be going. See, my betrayer is at hand."

In the voyage of life, there are junctures where the weight of the world feels unbearable. Moments when despair eclipses hope and the spirit feels utterly crushed. Some call it a breaking point. In such moments, it is not uncommon to wish for an end, to crave release from the torment. Many find themselves at the brink, feeling caged and overcome by the relentless waves of life's trials.

Our Savior, in His humanity, traversed through this valley of shadows. In the hushed whispers of olive trees at Gethsemane, He embodied the profound agony and distress that sears the human soul. It's a place I personally connected with during a transformative visit in 2008, where I stood amidst the ancient trees and felt the raw resonance of the name Gethsemane - a place of crushing.

In this garden, which once echoed with the silent cries of our Lord, we find a blueprint for navigating our darkest hours. All four gospels record, the olive press of Gethsemane, a place where olives were crushed to yield oil, mirrors the pressing anguish Jesus endured, a foreshadowing of the betrayals and suffering awaiting Him. When the pressures of life threaten to crush us, how should we respond?

Pray to the Father.

And going a little farther, He threw himself on the ground and prayed, "My Father."

Overwhelmed is a word that conveys the image of deep grief and sorrow. The song writer says: *"When my heart is overwhelmed, lead me to the rock that is higher than I."*

Be encouraged to find God, and to call on God.

If prayer is communing with God, which involves communication that manifests in conversation with God, then that is what we should be doing whenever we are feeling overwhelmed. We should turn to God. It seems that we find it easier to talk to all sorts of people, except God. If we are talking to all sorts of people, except God, then we are listening to all sorts of people except God.

There is nothing wrong in talking to people you trust, in seeking advice from others, in getting opinions and thoughts from people. Yet, we have a God who is available to us 24/7. A God in whom you can unburden your heart and find solace. He is always willing to listen to our deepest fears and hopes.

Let us not neglect this precious channel of grace, a direct line to divine guidance and peace. The late Barbadian Gospel artiste, Joseph Niles, considered by many to be the father of gospel in Barbados, reminded individuals of Jesus' availability so many times, in his song, "Royal Telephone:"

> *Central's never "busy," always on the line;*
> *You may hear from heaven almost any time;*
> *'Tis a royal service, free for one and all;*
> *When you get in trouble, give this royal line a call.*

Refrain:
Telephone to glory, oh, what joy divine!
I can feel the current moving on the line,
Built by God the Father for His loved and own,
We may talk to Jesus through this royal telephone.
2 There will be no charges, telephone is free,
It was built for service, just for you and me;
There will be no waiting on this royal line,
Telephone to glory always answers just in time. [Refrain]

Consider that Jesus in teaching His disciples how to pray said, **"Pray in this way: Our Father."**

It is to God that we look and turn to. It is to God that we address our needs, wants, desires and petitions. There are times then, when we must pray alone.

The disciples couldn't stay awake to pray, but that didn't stop Jesus from praying. Yet, for some of us, if certain people don't pray- no prayer happens. Some of us come to church and sing, read, clap and talk. But let's ask, "Can someone say the opening prayer?" Sometimes we have to wait five minutes. Don't let it be a large crowd. You will hear, "Pastor, you pray."

I encourage you to be courageous, bold and confident to talk to God. We can boldly approach our Father. He is a friend and brother even though He is a King. We need not be scared or afraid. God cares about us.

So, whether you are with others or by yourself, you are still praying to God.

1. Pray Honestly To God

"My Father, if it is possible, let this cup pass from me."

This is Jesus, the Son of God, the Messiah, the Saviour of the world, the one who cast out demons, healed the sick, and fed the 5 000. Jesus is asking for this cup to pass from Him. You cannot get more frank than that. Yet His honest plea is not just a moment of frankness but a teaching moment that uncovers the depth of his human experience.

In your times of overwhelming feelings, remember that God welcomes your honest expressions. Be honest with God. Tell Him how you feel and listen to Him. God is big enough and mature enough to hear our problems. Don't hold back. Don't pretend. Just as I observed in the church I grew up in, where evenings were filled with hymns of faith that resounded with heartfelt pleas and honest conversations with Jesus, you too can find solace in candid dialogues with God. The women would sing this hymn of faith, and repeat the chorus over and over and over:

Verse 3:
I may have doubts and fears, my eyes be filled with tears
But Jesus is a friend who watches day and night;
I go to him in prayer, He knows my every care
And just a little talk with Jesus makes it right

Chorus:
Now let us, Have a little talk with Jesus
Let us, tell Him all about our troubles
He will, Hear our faintest cry
And He will, answer by and by;

Now when you, feel a little prayer wheel turning
And you, know a little fire is burning
You will, find a little talk with Jesus makes it right.

Don't get it mixed up. There are no big or fancy words. Just a speech from the heart.

Don't get it mixed up. It does not have to be a two-hour prayer. The focus is not on the length of time, but prayer, a simple, heartfelt plea, like that of the Psalmist in Psalm 13, can echo the deepest corners of your soul:.

How long, O Lord? Will you forget me forever?
How long will you hide your face from me?
2 How long must I bear pain[a] in my soul,
and have sorrow in my heart all day long?
How long shall my enemy be exalted over me?

3 Consider and answer me, O Lord my God!
Give light to my eyes, or I will sleep the sleep of death,
4 and my enemy will say, "I have prevailed";
my foes will rejoice because I am shaken.

That's where many people are sometimes. They are overwhelmed. They ask, "God when will it end?" "When will it change?" "I cannot see, feel or hear you right now God!" Have You forgotten me? "I see everybody else is getting through, going ahead, but what about me?"

Pray honest prayers to God. When it gets too much, prayer to God.

2. Pray And Surrender To God

The embodiment of surrendering to God's will can be found in Jesus' heartfelt prayers during his moments of anguish. He prayed fervently, surrendering His desires and aligning His will with that of God's.

Jesus prayed, **"My Father, if it is possible, may this cup be taken from Me. Yet not as I will, but as You will."**

> [39] **And going a little farther, He threw himself on the ground and prayed, "My Father, if it is possible, let this cup pass from Me; yet not what I want but what You want."**

> [42] **Again He went away for the second time and prayed, "My Father, if this cannot pass unless I drink it, Your will be done."**

He went away and prayed for the third time, saying the same words. Three times Jesus prays, **"Not My will, but Your will."** Not my wants but Your wants, Lord. Not my way but Your way, Lord. Jesus vividly portrays the essence of surrendering to God, an act that transcends merely vocalizing our needs and wants. It is a profound act of humility and trust, where we let go of our desires, to embrace what God envisions for us. It's a dialogue where we keenly listen to God, seeking His guidance and entrusting our paths to Him.

Prayer it not one sided. It cannot always be about my needs, my wants or my problems only. We must surrender to the Lord and listen to the Sovereign Lord. Sing to the Lord. Down on my knees I talk with Jesus. Down on my knees I promised Jesus that I would serve Him, down on my knees.

"When Your Spirit speaks to me, with my whole heart I'll agree and my answer will be yes, Lord yes!

What do we pray in the **Lord's Prayer**? We say, "**Thy will be done on earth as it is in heaven.**"

May the will of God be done in your life, in this moment, in this season. May you surrender to the will and way of the Lord God Almighty.

What is the revelation or confirmation that you are hearing and receiving from God? May there be clarity for you to hear God's voice.

One of the reasons why some of us are so dependent on other people, is that we have not developed the discipline of sitting before the Lord, spending time in His presence, and being still, as we wait on Him. In your prayer journey, I encourage you to cultivate the habit of stillness, to discern God's voice amidst the noise and to surrender fully to His will. Develop a discipline of sitting quietly in God's presence, allowing His voice to guide your steps, indicating when to pause and when to forge ahead.

In our journey of faith, hymns have been a source of comfort and strength, echoing the sentiments of surrender and trust in God. We often find ourselves immersed in these words:

What a Friend we have in Jesus,
All our sins and griefs to bear!
What a privilege to carry
Everything to God in prayer!
Oh, what peace we often forfeit,
Oh, what needless pain we bear,
All because we do not carry
Everything to God in prayer!

Have we trials and temptations?
Is there trouble anywhere?
We should never be discouraged—
Take it to the Lord in prayer.
Can we find a Friend so faithful,
Who will all our sorrows share?
Jesus knows our every weakness;
Take it to the Lord in prayer.

Are we weak and heavy-laden,
Cumbered with a load of care?
Precious Saviour, still our refuge—
Take it to the Lord in prayer.
Do thy friends despise, forsake thee?
Take it to the Lord in prayer!
In His arms He'll take and shield thee,
Thou wilt find a solace there.

Remember, the God who has seen through generations, who knows our past and future, is ever ready to guide us. In times of overwhelming burdens, let us take a leaf from Jesus' book - praying honestly and surrendering wholly to God, fully trusting in His divine orchestration. When it seems too much, find your refuge in honest prayers and complete surrender to God, who holds our best interests at heart.

Jesus, during his time of distress, did not just pray and surrender; He also arose and stepped forth to face the inevitable, illustrating the vital principle that prayer should lead to decisive action.

3. Pray And Step Forth With God

45 Then He came to the disciples and said to them, "Are you still sleeping and taking your rest? See, the hour is at hand, and the Son of Man is betrayed into the hands of sinners. 46 Get up, let us be going. See, My betrayer is at hand."

Understanding the seasons and timings is vital in our walk with Jesus. As Ecclesiastes 3:1 underscores, **For everything there is a season, and a time for every matter under heaven..."** If you do not understand seasons, you will mess things up and miss some things. These pivotal moments often call for us to rise and align our spirits harmoniously with God, ready to act according to His guidance and the prompting of the Holy Spirit.

Jesus asked His disciples, **"Are you still sleeping and taking rest?"**

Unfortunately, many find themselves spiritually asleep, bogged down by petty conflicts and distractions, at a time when decisive action is required. The escalating darkness in the world necessitates a community, a church that is awake, ready to step forward with God to enact positive change.

Prayer doesn't just provide solace; it equips us with the courage and resolve to face our daily challenges head-on. **"Rise, let us go! Here comes My betrayer!"** Jesus said.

If we continue with the reading, here is what it says:

⁴⁷ While He was still speaking, Judas, one of the twelve, arrived; with Him was a large crowd with swords and clubs, from the chief priests and the elders of the people.

⁴⁸ Now the betrayer had given them a sign, saying, "The One I will kiss is the man; arrest him." ⁴⁹ At once he came up to Jesus and said, "Greetings, Rabbi!" and kissed Him. ⁵⁰ Jesus said to him, "Friend, do what you are here to do." Then they came and laid hands on Jesus and arrested Him.

Whether it is navigating a hostile work environment, mending familial ties, or confronting gossip and slander, prayer fortifies us, providing the strength to face these situations with grace and dignity. As you navigate these challenges, carry the spirit of prayer with you. Let it be a source of continual peace and resolve. And in moments when you find yourself awaiting the sweet hour of prayer, remember these comforting words:

Sweet hour of prayer! Sweet hour of prayer!
That calls me from a world of care,
And bids me at my Father's throne
Make all my wants and wishes known.
In seasons of distress and grief,
My soul has often found relief,
And oft escaped the tempter's snare,
By thy return, sweet hour of prayer!
Sweet hour of prayer! Sweet hour of prayer!
Thy wings shall my petition bear
To Him whose truth and faithfulness
Engage the waiting soul to bless.
And since He bids me seek His face,
Believe His Word and trust His grace,
I'll cast on Him my every care,
And wait for thee, sweet hour of prayer!

Let these words be your rallying cry, a reminder of the unyielding support and guidance that prayer provides. So, in times of overwhelm, turn to God with honest prayers, surrender to His will, and step forth boldly, hand in hand with the Almighty, ready to face whatever comes your way.

WHEN THEY LOOK DOWN ON YOU – HAVE CONFIDENCE

1 Samuel 17: 28-49

28 His eldest brother Eliab heard him talking to the men, and Eliab's anger was kindled against David. He said, "Why have you come down? With whom have you left those few sheep in the wilderness? I know your presumption and the evil of your heart, for you have come down just to see the battle." 29 David said, "What have I done now? It was only a question." 30 He turned away from him toward another and spoke in the same way, and the people answered him again as before.

31 When the words that David spoke were heard, they repeated them before Saul, and he sent for him. 32 David said to Saul, "Let no one's heart fail because of him; your servant will go and fight with this Philistine." 33 Saul said to David, "You are not able to go against this Philistine

to fight with him, for you are just a boy, and he has been a warrior from his youth." 34 But David said to Saul, "Your servant used to keep sheep for his father, and whenever a lion or a bear came and took a lamb from the flock, 35 I went after it and struck it down, rescuing the lamb from its mouth, and if it turned against me, I would catch it by the jaw, strike it down, and kill it. 36 Your servant has killed both lions and bears, and this uncircumcised Philistine shall be like one of them, since he has defied the armies of the living God." 37 David said, "The Lord, who saved me from the paw of the lion and from the paw of the bear, will save me from the hand of this Philistine." So Saul said to David, "Go, and may the Lord be with you!"

38 Saul clothed David with his armor; he put a bronze helmet on his head and clothed him with a coat of mail. 39 David strapped Saul's sword over the armor, and he tried in vain to walk, for he was not used to them. Then David said to Saul, "I cannot walk with these, for I am not used to them." So David removed them. 40 Then he took his staff in his hand and chose five smooth stones from the wadi and put them in his shepherd's bag, in the

pouch; his sling was in his hand, and he
drew near to the Philistine.

41 The Philistine came on and drew near
to David, with his shield-bearer in front
of him. 42 When the Philistine looked
and saw David, he disdained him, for he
was only a youth, ruddy and handsome
in appearance. 43 The Philistine said to
David, "Am I a dog, that you come to
me with sticks?" And the Philistine cursed
David by his gods. 44 The Philistine said
to David, "Come to me, and I will give
your flesh to the birds of the air and to the
wild animals of the field." 45 But David
said to the Philistine, "You come to me
with sword and spear and javelin, but I
come to you in the name of the Lord of
hosts, the God of the armies of Israel,
whom you have defied. 46 This very day
the Lord will deliver you into my hand,
and I will strike you down and cut off
your head, and I will give the dead bodies
of the Philistine army this very day to the
birds of the air and to the wild animals of
the earth, so that all the earth may know
that there is a God in Israel 47 and that
all this assembly may know that the Lord
does not save by sword and spear, for the
battle is the Lord's, and he will give you
into our hand."

48 When the Philistine drew nearer to meet David, David ran quickly toward the battle line to meet the Philistine. 49 David put his hand in his bag, took out a stone, slung it, and struck the Philistine on his forehead; the stone sank into his forehead, and he fell face down on the ground.

In the heart of the battlefield, where the stench of fear and uncertainty permeated the air, the army of Israel stood paralyzed. A formidable figure had managed to instill a deep-seated fear in the hearts of the trained and equipped soldiers of Israel. You might wonder, why was an entire army shaking in fear?

The reason stood nearly 10 feet tall, an intimidating giant named Goliath of Gath who emerged from the Philistine camp, his mere presence commanding attention and instilling dread. In this atmosphere thick with trepidation, a young shepherd boy named David found himself confronting not only the giant but also the dismissive and disparaging views of those around him. Whether you are an adult or young person reading this book, we sometimes go through a crisis of people looking down on us.

For some of us, this is troubling, disturbing, painful and frustrating. We wonder why. David's story reveals that:

They look down because not everybody will like you.

Jesse had eight sons. The eldest brother, Eliab, couldn't hide his jealousy or disdain for the future king. After all, he was the eldest of Jesse's sons. Shouldn't he have been anointed king?

It might be family, co-workers, other children in the class, those on the same team as you, those in the same church, ministry, or choir, some people just don't and won't like you.

You might come across people who cannot hide their negative feelings towards you. Unfortunately, you cannot be liked by everyone.

They don't like how you speak or how you look. To them you are either too fat, too slim, too tall, too short, or they do not like the clothes you are wearing. Simple things such as, they do not like the blue jeans or the dress you are wearing; they do not like your hairstyle, or that Brazilian weave you are wearing. Even when you do your best, some laugh and make fun at you. Remember their perception is not your reality.

They look down on you because not everybody can handle you. They look down on you because they simply may not be on your side. That's okay. Not everyone can handle the potential and the gifts that you possess. Your abilities might be a mirror reflecting their shortcomings, which can often lead to envy and resentment. Not everyone was on David's side. Not everyone was on Jesus's side. But neither of them, walked away from their calling. They did not back away from what God called them to. So don't you back away or run away from your calling, don't let the naysayers deter you. David faced disdain and humiliation from his brother.

> **28 But when David's oldest brother, Eliab, heard David talking to the men, he was angry. "What are you doing around here anyway?" he demanded. "What about those few sheep you're supposed to be taking care of? I know about your pride and deceit. You just want to see the battle!"**
>
> **29 "What have I done now?" David replied. "I was only asking a question!" (NLT)**

Very often people attempt to silence those they look down on. Some individuals may try to suppress your voice. They might attempt to hinder your efforts to assist others. Your skills, gifts, or talents can sometimes be viewed as threats rather than assets.

So, people will look down on you, doubt you and talk down to you.

David was a young boy. He was untrained. If he possessed any training, it was as a result of tending sheep. He was not by any means a fighter, but he had more courage than the soldiers or the king. Youthful vigor and innocence can sometimes unmask the weaknesses and failures of those who underestimate you. That is why Paul admonishes: **"Let no one despise your youth."**

If you are a child, be a child. Enjoy your childhood. You won't always be young. When you enter that stage of adulthood you cannot go back to being a child.

As a youth, when they look down on you, remember to stand tall, firm in your faith and the unique gifts God has bestowed upon you. Harness the youthful energy, the freshness of perspective, and the courage that comes with it to face the Goliaths in your life. After all, in the grand scheme of things, it's not the opinion of the naysayers that matters, but the purpose and plan that God has set for you.

1. Step up with boldness

For 40 days the Philistine came forward every morning and evening and took his stand.

To step up with boldness is to step up and do the small tasks.

¹⁷ Jesse said to his son David, "Take for your brothers an ephah of this parched

grain and these ten loaves, and carry them quickly to the camp to your brothers; ¹⁸ also take these ten cheeses to the commander of their thousand. See how your brothers fare, and bring some token from them."

¹⁹ Now Saul, and they, and all the men of Israel were in the valley of Elah fighting with the Philistines. ²⁰ David rose early in the morning, left the sheep with a keeper, took the provisions, and went as Jesse had commanded him.

It was David's adherence to his father's words, his readiness to undertake what might have seemed a menial task, that placed him in the pivotal position to confront and conquer Goliath. Some of you may be saying, "They are always asking me to do this and that.", sometimes feeling overwhelmed by the incessant demands of others. Remember, the tasks that seem insignificant could be shaping stones, preparing you for greater challenges ahead.

In the case of fighting Goliath, nobody stepped up because everybody was afraid.

²⁴ As soon as the Israelite army saw him, they began to run away in fright. ²⁵ "Have you seen the giant?" the men asked. "He comes out each day to defy Israel. (NLT)

At a time where fear paralyzed even the bravest, no one dared to confront Goliath, despite the lavish rewards (wealth, marriage to his daughter, and freedom) promised by King Saul. It was here that the concept of boldness, a quality deeply

REV. DR. ADRIAN SMITH

grounded in faith and conviction, comes into play. Boldness is acting by the power of the Holy Spirit, on an urgent conviction in the face of some threat. Boldness is fearlessness because of confidence in God. It is because of the confidence in God that there is no worry or fear about the potential consequences.

We who are Christians must also take to heart that to be bold does not mean to be disrespectful. Dr. Richard J Krejcir aptly encapsulates this sentiment when he states, "Boldness is our willingness to venture out and do the right thing at the right time, regardless of the barriers or fears we may encounter. This enables us to speak the truth, and perform a task without fear of the consequences or results, because, it is the right, and Biblical thing to do. It is realizing that God is in control. He is there within, and beside us, and He will take care of us. Therefore, we do not need to fear what others can do; rather, we are to concentrate on our character and call, and do it with passion and conviction."[4]

However, boldness is not an attribute that manifests without a deep-seated conviction and a sense of urgency. It requires a fire, a driving force that propels you forward, to act and speak without hesitation as in Acts 4: **"[29] And now, Lord, look at their threats, and grant to your servants to speak your word with all boldness, [30] while you stretch out your hand to heal, and signs and wonders are performed through the name of your holy servant[k] Jesus." [31] When they had prayed, the place in which they were gathered together was shaken, and they were all filled with the Holy Spirit and spoke the word of God with boldness. (Acts 4:29,31)**

In the face of adversity and disparagement, may you find the courage to step up with boldness, embracing the tasks and opportunities that lay before you with a heart grounded in faith and conviction. Remember, when they look down on you, it's your time to rise, to step up with a boldness that is grounded in the very spirit of God at work within you.

2. Stand up with courage

"Courage is not simply one of the virtues, but the form of every virtue at the testing point," noted C.S. Lewis, emphasizing that courage is the underpinning of all virtuous actions, particularly when faced with fear or adversity. Courage signifies not the absence of fear, but the fortitude to face it. It is a potent blend of strength and discernment, where one stands tall without resorting to reckless or destructive behaviors.

David's declaration to Goliath rings as a timeless testament to divine courage, "You come against me with sword and spear and javelin, but I come against you in the name of the Lord Almighty, the God of the armies of Israel, whom you have defied." David confronted the giant Goliath with a courage fueled by an unwavering faith in God.

Stand up! Face others and the things no one else wants to face.

This faith-infused courage empowers us to face life's formidable giants, to stand alone if necessary, against oppositions that seem insurmountable. Goliath, a towering figure, shielded and armed to the teeth, had held the entire Israelite army at bay for forty days. Yet, young David chose to step forward, not deterred by Goliath's physical might or his undefeated status.

As you are reading this, you might be called upon to take the first step up, to take the initiative and go; to do what no one else wants to do. It's easy to criticize others for their inactions, but perhaps, God is stirring a spirit of boldness within you to act, to face those unbeaten 'Goliaths'.

It is easy and might be justifiable to grumble and complain about everyone who has not done or is not doing what they are supposed to do. You are right. It probably should not be you doing it; who is doing everything. But alas, God has given you that spirit of boldness – the agitation in your heart to do something. History and scriptures alike teach us that with God, the 'impossible' is possible. Like the Gracehill Moravian Church in Barbados aptly expresses, we are "Serving a God of Endless Possibilities."

As you navigate your journey, dare to try different approaches, to innovate, and to follow your convictions. Is doing things differently one of the reasons we can triumph and overcome? Well, you won't know until you try. So, try a different approach. Try something new. Try what your heart tells you to try. Try what God tells you. The scripture is replete with accounts of unconventional strategies God instructed His people to employ, leading them to victory. Put the trumpeters, the singers, before the army. Dip in a dirty river (yeah, I know it was the Jordan River). Use some disciples with questionable skills and backgrounds. Imagine Judas and Peter? Don't talk about Saul! Take a cue from these narratives; don't shy away from trying what God places on your heart.

Remember the encouraging words in **Joshua 1:9 (NLT), "Be strong and courageous! Do not be afraid or discouraged and find further affirmation in Psalm 31:24(NLT), "So be strong and courageous, all you who put your hope in the Lord!**

When faced with disdain or discouragement, remember to step up with boldness, stand up with courage, and speak up with confidence.

3. Speak Up - Confidence

Confidence is not just an innate sense of self-assurance, but a deep-rooted conviction in who you are in God, aligned with your divine purpose and destiny. It transcends the belief in one's abilities, manifesting as a radiant light that captures the attention and admiration of others, even amidst criticism. It's a voice that resounds with clarity and conviction, a force that propels you to venture where others might hesitate, drawing from a reservoir of faith and past experiences.

David, a young shepherd, was unafraid to voice his courage and faith in the face of a formidable enemy. His words weren't just utterances, but a testament to his experiences and steadfast belief in God's deliverance. "whenever a lion or a bear came and took a lamb from the flock, [35] I went after it and struck it down..." (1 Samuel 17:34-35).

Speak up with confidence and do your best.

David's conviction was not baseless; it stemmed from a history of God's protection and guidance. Each time David spoke, his words caught the attention of someone else.

[31] What David said was overheard and reported to Saul, and Saul sent for him.

[32] David said to Saul, "Let no one lose heart on account of this Philistine; your servant will go and fight him."

This positioned him, higher and higher. Like David, you have unique experiences and insights to bring to the table, fresh perspectives that can revolutionize old paradigms. When you speak with the wisdom of your experiences, coupled with a firm belief in God's hand in your life, the right people will sit up and take notice. People admire persons with confidence, even if they criticise them. When you speak with confidence the right people will hear and notice you. You don't know- who is hearing you sing, watching you play sports, or watching you act.

David spoke to the king

> ³⁴ But David said to Saul, "Your servant used to keep sheep for his father, and whenever a lion or a bear came and took a lamb from the flock, ³⁵ I went after it and struck it down, rescuing the lamb from its mouth, and if it turned against me, I would catch it by the jaw, strike it down, and kill it. ³⁶ Your servant has killed both lions and bears, and this uncircumcised Philistine shall be like one of them, since he has defied the armies of the living God." ³⁷ David said, "The Lord, who saved me from the paw of the lion and from the paw of the bear, will save me from the hand of this Philistine."

> Saul said to David, "Go, and may the Lord be with you."

> ⁴⁵ But David said to the Philistine, "You come to me with sword and spear and javelin, but I come to you in the name of the Lord of hosts, the God of the armies of Israel, whom you have defied. ⁴⁶ This very day the Lord will deliver you into my hand

That was his story, his experiences, out of which he believed that the same God was on his side and would do again what he did before.

I declare over your life and situation right now, that your God, our God, is ready to do the same in your life and He will do again what he did before demonstrating His power and faithfulness. In Jesus' name.

But remember, speaking with confidence is only part of the equation. Much like David, we must also act with a bold assurance, ready to meet challenges head-on with a spirit of victory. **[48] When the Philistine drew nearer to meet David, David ran quickly toward the battle line to meet the Philistine. [49] David put his hand in his bag, took out a stone, slung it, and struck the Philistine on his forehead; the stone sank into his forehead, and he fell face down on the ground.**

Yet, confidence is not merely a display of words but is exhibited in action. David demonstrated this as he ran swiftly towards Goliath, a beacon of fearless confidence and divine assurance. His actions echoed a profound trust in God, unshaken by the towering challenges that stood before him.

David encouraged himself in the Lord

Confidence in what God did in the past, God saved, rescued, and delivered David

David did not apologise for his faith. He stepped up and stepped out. Stop apologising because you believe, because you are so confident, courageous, energetic and ready to go. This is the essence of speaking up with confidence - a melding of past experiences, an unwavering faith, and a readiness to step into the role God has carved out for you.

Paul told Timothy to be an example to the believer in thought, word, speech, and in conduct. Paul further reminds us that "I can do all things through Christ who strengthens me." (Philippians 4:13)

When we step up, stand up and speak up, we will stand out. You may feel that you do not fit in anywhere or with any group. But God will stand with you. So, no matter how people feel about you, what they think about you, how they talk about you, hold your head up, be bold, confident, courageous, and go forward in the name of the Lord.

What an encouraging and empowering testimony we have from David. We have to know that the Living God created us for our specific purposes. When we go to Him, He will propel us into our future. We will come up against enemies, our Goliaths, our Philistines, who for whatever reason want us to back down against their standing, their words, and their strengths. They are nothing, when we like David boldly go before them in the name of the Lord. Literally. We must keep the prayer and words David used in on our hearts and minds and use them to bring down our Goliaths.

Much like David, I found myself in a moment where stepping up with confidence was not just an option but a necessity. As the leader of our church's regional Synod (highest decision-making authority of our regional province), a role of great responsibility and honor, I felt a whirlwind of nerves and apprehension engulf me. In the cool confines of an air-conditioned room, my palms sweated, and my stomach churned with unease. I was sweating, feeling hot in an air-conditioned room, and wondering if I needed glasses because all of a sudden, I couldn't see people in the back of the room, then I realised the situation I was in.

People assume that because you speak or preach in public that you do not get nervous or scared. I remember reading the church's constitution and Roberts Rule of Order repeatedly. It was then that I realized the necessity to transcend my physical sensations, to entrust myself and the moment into God's capable hands, seeking His guidance and strength. "Do not fear, for I am with you; do not be afraid, for I am your God; I will strengthen you; I will help you; I will uphold you with my victorious right hand." (Isaiah 41:10).

David's story beckons us to embody this level of confidence, to boldly step before our own 'Goliaths' with a conviction that victory is assured in the name of the Lord. Even when facing adversaries who seemingly tower over us, with God by our side, victory is assured. Remember, when you embody this form of divine confidence, not only do you stand up, but you also stand out.

As you traverse your journey, may you carry with you the assurance that, despite the voices of doubt or critique, God stands firmly with you. In the grand scheme of things, it matters not how others perceive you. Equip yourself with the prayers and words that David held close to his heart, ready to bring down your Goliaths. Stand tall, speak with confidence, and move forward in the mighty name of the Lord, for in Him, you are more than a conqueror.

WHEN PEOPLE
ABANDON YOU – FIND
STRENGTH IN GOD

Matthew Chapter 26:55-68

> 55 At that hour Jesus said to the crowds,
> "Have you come out with swords and clubs
> to arrest me as though I were a rebel? Day
> after day I sat in the temple teaching, and
> you did not arrest me. 56 But all this has
> taken place, so that the scriptures of the
> prophets may be fulfilled." Then all the
> disciples deserted him and fled.

Jesus before the High Priest

> 57 Those who had arrested Jesus took him
> to Caiaphas the high priest, where the
> scribes and the elders had gathered. 58
> But Peter was following him at a distance,
> as far as the courtyard of the high priest,
> and going inside he sat with the guards in
> order to see how this would end. 59 Now

the chief priests and the whole council were looking for false testimony against Jesus so that they might put him to death, 60 but they found none, though many false witnesses came forward. At last two came forward 61 and said, "This fellow said, 'I am able to destroy the temple of God and to build it in three days.'" 62 The high priest stood up and said, "Have you no answer? What is it that they testify against you?" 63 But Jesus was silent. Then the high priest said to him, "I put you under oath before the living God, tell us if you are the Messiah,[a] the Son of God." 64 Jesus said to him, "You have said so. But I tell you,

From now on you will see the Son of Man
    seated at the right hand of Power
    and coming on the clouds of heaven."

65 Then the high priest tore his clothes and said, "He has blasphemed! Why do we still need witnesses? You have now heard his blasphemy. 66 What do you think?" They answered, "He deserves death." 67 Then they spat in his face and struck him, and some slapped him, 68 saying, "Prophesy to us, you Messiah![b] Who is it that struck you?"

Most of the difficulties we have in life are people related, people centred and people driven. It was people who killed

Jesus. People! All four Gospels (Matthew Chapter 26:30-75; Mark Chapter 14:26-72; Luke Chapter 22:31-71; John Chapter 8:1-27) capture the story of how Jesus was treated the last week before He died.

In this passage, we witness a heart-breaking scene: Jesus, the Savior, is deserted by His disciples— the ones who journeyed with him for three years, the ones in whom He saw potential even when they didn't see it in themselves, those who had been His companions and confidantes, they all deserted him and fled.

The term 'abandonment' is strong, laden with implications of forsaking and renouncing allegiance. Dictionary definitions indicate that to abandon is to give up absolutely; to forsake entirely ; to renounce utterly; to relinquish all connection with or concern on; to desert, to leave alone; to desert as a person to whom one owes allegiance or fidelity; to leave behind or run away from someone or something, or to give up something: to quit; to surrender, to leave someone, especially someone you are responsible for, with no intention of returning.[5]

Life often mirrors this scriptural tableau, with loved ones and confidantes distancing themselves in times of peril. People abandon you out of fear. They abandon you for self-preservation. They save themselves. If Jesus experienced this type of abandonment from those He was closest to, in His time here on earth, won't we as well experience similar times, sometimes from the ones we poured the most into? But alas, Jesus' perspective was not one of Him acting or of Him being the victim continuously. He acknowledged his disappointment. He knew it was all for a specific purpose. It is important to be honest with yourself and moreover, to be honest with God who, is the Author and Perfecter of your faith. He knows times of abandonment and disappointment will come. He also sees beyond them.

What do you do when people abandon you? Times when your family, friends, co-workers, even your church brothers and sisters abandon you? You must find strength in God.

According to Richard Patterson, "When we think of the concept of strength, we most commonly associate it with physical power. Yet, strength and power are overlapping synonyms, which carry the sense of an inherent capacity to be able to act effectively, whether physically, intellectually, or morally."[6]

It is the reason the Apostle Paul is able to say, **"I can do all things."** We are also told to be strong in the Lord, for it is God who gives strength, power and might.

1. Find Strength By Staying Focused On God's Will

[57] Those who had arrested Jesus took him to Caiaphas the high priest, where the teachers of the law and the elders had assembled.

The Gospel of Mark says- **[53] They took Jesus to the high priest, and all the chief priests, the elders and the teachers of the law came together.**

It is Luke's Gospel that tells us, **[54] Then seizing Him, they led Him away and took Him into the house of the high priest.**

The Great Sanhedrin in Jerusalem was made up of 71 men including the high priest, chief priests, elders and scribes. This group was also called, "the council of the elders," and "the senate of the sons of Israel."

It was a conspiracy based on who was there.

It was a conspiracy based on the time it occurred; it was night.

It was a conspiracy based on where it was; in Caiaphas house.

It's was a conspiracy based on what they were doing. They were soliciting charges against Jesus rather than responding to charges already made.

What was the basis of the arrest? Everything about it was wrong.

We experience it sometimes in church. They have meetings before the meetings and meetings after the meeting. Then you hear someone say, "I was thinking." You weren't thinking, you were influenced, coerced to change your mind, and you were prejudiced. They were trying to set you up to fail, to look bad and make themselves sound intelligent and look good. Yet, I encourage you to stay focused. All things happen as a part of God's will and a part of His divine plan. It is also important to remember when various types of situations attempt to aid you to compromise your beliefs, the Bible says in **Psalm 51:10-12: "Create in me a clean heart, O God, and put a new and right spirit within me. Do not cast me away from your presence, and do not take your Holy Spirit from me. Restore to me the joy of your salvation, and sustain in me a willing spirit."**

This verse can aid tremendously in helping us to traverse such types of situations. Keeping these words on our lips can guide our hearts and minds. Availing ourselves to this type of introspection with God can bring the right view to situations which can be murky.

Stay Focused Even Though the Disciples Are Sitting With Guards- Maliciousness

> **⁵⁸ But Peter followed Him at a distance, right up to the courtyard of the high priest. He entered and sat down with the guards to see the outcome.**

Peter followed, but from a distance. You have some people around you, in your life, who follow your **Facebook** page but they do not comment. They follow you on **Instagram (IG)** also. They want your cell number to see your status, to see who your beau is and to see with whom and where you take pictures. They are malicious.

It's a case of no public support. No public loyalty. Sitting with the enemy! Peter was not just one of the disciples; he was part of the inner crew. Where is he now?

Stay Focused Even Though People Are Coming Forward Lying- Deviousness

> **⁵⁹ The chief priests and the whole Sanhedrin were looking for false evidence against Jesus so that they could put Him to death. ⁶⁰ But they did not find any, though many false witnesses came forward.**

A conviction could only be made upon the testimony of two or more reliable witnesses. These witnesses had to affirm their testimony was true to the best of their knowledge and was based on their own direct experience and not on hearsay or presumption.

My grandmother and other seniors would always say that the only thing worse than a thief is a liar. If and when you open your mouth to say a half-truth, quarter truth or delayed truth- you are lying. From the moment you open your mouth, let truth come out. In our world there is an abundance of spin doctors and fake news. So many persons do not know what to believe or who to believe. I encourage you through the lyrics of the song by Hezekiah Walker, titled, **God favoured Me"**

They whispered, conspired, they told their lies (God favours me)
My character, my integrity, my faith in God (He favours me)
Will not fall, will not bend, won't compromise (God favours me)
I speak life and prosperity and I speak health (God favours me)

When they abandon you find strength by staying focused on God's will.

2. Find Strength By Staying Faithful To God's Word

> [62] Then the high priest stood up and said to Jesus, "Are you not going to answer? What is this testimony that these men are bringing against you?" [63] But Jesus remained silent.
>
> The high priest said to Him, "I charge you under oath by the living God: Tell us if you are the Messiah, the Son of God."
>
> [64] "You have said so," Jesus replied. "But I say to all of you: From now on you will see the Son of Man sitting at the right

hand of the Mighty One and coming on the clouds of heaven."[e]

65 Then the high priest tore His clothes and said, "He has spoken blasphemy! Why do we need any more witnesses? Look, now you have heard the blasphemy. 66 What do you think?"

"He is worthy of death," they answered.

67 Then they spit in His face and struck Him with their fists. Others slapped Him 68 and said, "Prophesy to us, Messiah. Who hit you?"

Stay Faithful To The Word Even Though Insulted

They interrogated Jesus and they mocked Him. So, it compounded what they were doing to Him and what some people will do to you. They conspire against you and lie on you. Then, to insult you, or as a friend of mine would say, "they trying to insult my intelligence."

From the time they insult some of us, we are through with them and that. We quit or resign.

"Don't call my name for nothing." "Don't ask for nothing." In fact, like some boys I played cricket with growing up, if you made fun at them or laughed at them, they would walk with the stumps, bat, and ball, because they were theirs.

You are encouraged to stay faithful though they insult you. Do it out of obedience to God, to please God and to fulfil the mission and assignment given to you.

Stay Faithful To The Word Even Though Inflicted

⁶⁵ Then some began to spit at Him; they blindfolded Him, struck Him with their fists, and said, "Prophesy!" And the guards took Him and beat Him.

In no way would I advocate anyone to take any form of physical abuse from anyone, anytime or anywhere. Let me make this clear. If you experience any form of physical abuse get help immediately. Go to the police. And if you witness or know of anyone who is being abused, report it to the authorities.

What the Scripture implores is faithfulness to God even if we suffer for righteousness' sake. We are forewarned that based on what they did to Jesus, we can expect the same to happen to His followers. There will be trials, people will betray, abandon, and turn on you. Some will lie on you, publicly ridicule, and persecute you.

There are persons who think that because you love God; because you are a follower of Jesus, because you attend church, that you are to be their doormat, a walkover, someone who is easy to push over. Always remember God's Word: **"Do not repay evil for evil...Vengeance is mine, says the Lord, I will repay."(Romans 12:17-21)**

Brace yourself. Prepare yourself. But stay faithful to God.

Stay Faithful To The Word
Even Though Indicted.

Isaiah 53

he had no form or majesty that we should look at him,
   nothing in his appearance that we should desire him.
³ He was despised and rejected by others;
   a man of suffering[a] and acquainted with infirmity,
and as one from whom others hide their faces[b]
   he was despised, and we held him of no account.

⁴ Surely he has borne our infirmities
   and carried our diseases,
yet we accounted him stricken,
   struck down by God, and afflicted.
⁵ But he was wounded for our transgressions,
   crushed for our iniquities;
upon him was the punishment that made us whole,
   and by his bruises we are healed.
⁶ All we like sheep have gone astray;
   we have all turned to our own way,
and the Lord has laid on him
   the iniquity of us all.

⁷ He was oppressed, and he was afflicted,
   yet he did not open his mouth;
like a lamb that is led to the slaughter
   and like a sheep that before its shearers is silent,
so he did not open his mouth.

Jesus was going to be arrested, put on trials, three trials in total. But He never backed down or looked back. He was beaten, disfigured, humiliated, stripped naked, dragged through the streets, nailed on the cross and He suffered excruciating pains. You know how we say it in church: They hung Him high, and stretch Him wide.

Yet, He cried out, **"It is finished."** It is done. The will of His Father was done. You know how this story ends. Early one Sunday morning, the stone was rolled away and up from the grave He rose. Hallelujah!

Because He lives, you can face tomorrow. Because he lives, all fear is gone. Because I know, I know He holds the future, and life is worth the living just because He lives.

In these difficult times, when you go through difficult times, when you are caught between a rock and a hard place with your back against a wall, you have to praise your way through.

They have abandoned you and scandalised your name. In the face of all this, don't stop praising God. Keep your praise. Praise more fervently. Praise more passionately attitude, and just praise God.

By now you must have come to the conclusion that I love music. I love songs and I love hymnody.

My dad cultivated my love for music. All genres of music. I love from Jimmy Cliff, Bob Marley and the Wailers, Eric Clapton, Queen, the Beatles to Jackie Opel, the Merrymen and the Troubadours - to name a few. He would collect vinyl records, L.P'S and E.P'S and every week, he would play them and have us singing along. But it was my paternal grandmother, Enid Smith, who would ignite the fire for Gospel music. She was the choir director for the Newbury Nazarene Church, and she would often hum some song in preparation for choir rehearsal or service. The joy of listening to her was that she would sometimes sing all four parts of the song. Music therefore became that soothing, calming impact to my life. The times I am flooded with inspiring thoughts to finish papers and sermons have been against the background of classical music, jazz and Gospel. My faith is expressed in the words of many songwriters. I bellow songs from my room, car or bathroom. Singing gave expression to the deepest feelings.

I have held on to the following quotes:

> *"Music gives a soul to the universe, wings to the mind, flight to the imagination, and life to everything."*
> *— Plato*

> "Where words fail, music speaks."
> — Hans Christian Andersen

Phil Thompson sings that beautiful song, titled, My Worship. It goes:

> *Here's my worship,*
> *all of my worship,*
> *receive my worship,*
> *all of my worship*
> *And I will not be silent*
> *I will always worship You*
> *As long as I am breathing*
> *I will always worship You*

When things run out, when we lose some things and some people lose everything, when things don't change, when it gets too much, when people look down on you, when everybody abandons you… what do you do? Trust God. Have hope, **faith and** determination. Pray. Find confidence and strength in

God. Encourage yourself in the Lord and keep praising God. Remember that it is impossible to please God without faith.

So, what does your faith looks like in any of the above situations? Faith is the assurance of things not yet seen, but hoped for? So, we must ask ourselves, how in this situation can I demonstrate such?

MOMENTS OF HOPE

Resilience: An Anchor in Uncertainty

Philippians 4:10-14

> [10] I rejoice[c] in the Lord greatly that now at last you have revived your concern for me; indeed, you were concerned for me, but had no opportunity to show it.[d] [11] Not that I am referring to being in need; for I have learned to be content with whatever I have. [12] I know what it is to have little, and I know what it is to have plenty. In any and all circumstances I have learned the secret of being well-fed and of going hungry, of having plenty and of being in need. [13] I can do all things through him who strengthens me. [14] In any case, it was kind of you to share my distress.

There is no doubt by now that 2020 will be remembered as the year of COVID-19 and the multiplicity of uncertainties this pandemic created. It created uncertainty about economies, tourism, health and safety, job sourcing and job security, normalcy (what is normal?) freedom, shutdowns and lockdowns.

COVID-19 changed what we thought was normal. It really caused all of us to embrace new things.

The need for resilience has never been more urgent. Resilience is characterised as: "the capacity and ability to recover quickly from difficulties, depression, illness and adversity. Resilience is our lifeline, the capacity that enables us to swiftly recover from difficulties, acting as our anchor amid life's stormy seas. In this time of change and unpredictability, resilience is not just toughness but a necessary trait for practicing faith amidst crisis.

Another dictionary's definition of resilience is: "the power or ability to return to the original form, position, etcetera… after being bent, compressed, or stretched, elasticity."

Are you feeling bent, stretched, frustrated or compressed by life's challenges? Here, I urge you to cultivate resilience.

1. A Resilient Mind Through Positive Thinking

Embrace the empowering adage "Yes, we can!" popularized by former President of the United States, Barack Obama, aligning with the Apostle Paul's assurance that "I can do all things through him (Christ) who gives me strength" (Philippians 4:13).

Positive thinking is crucial to resilience, helping to navigate through pain and negativity. Renew your mind continually, aligning it with God's will, and believe in yourself, staying hopeful and confident in God.

Keep Believing In Yourself- Back yourself!

A resilient mind can push pass the conformities, cultures, and conditioning. A resilient mind can help get us get to the place of achieving our goals. A resilient mind can help us believe where our faith wants to carry us. It is why the Apostle Paul invites us to think about… **Fix your thoughts on what is true, and honorable, and right, and pure, and lovely, and admirable. Think about things that are excellent and worthy of praise. Philippians 4:8 (NLT)**

This tells me that while we may be beset by what happened to us, we can still determine where we keep our mind and what it keeps focussed on. A resilient mind is confident and full of hope in God. **37 No, despite all these things, overwhelming victory is ours through Christ, who loved us. 38 And I am convinced that nothing can ever separate us from God's love. Neither death nor life, neither angels nor demons, [p] neither our fears for today nor our worries about tomorrow—not even the powers of hell can separate us from God's love. 39 No power in the sky above or in the earth below—indeed, nothing in all creation will ever be able to separate us from the love of God that is revealed in Christ Jesus our Lord. Romans 8:37-39 (NLT)**

Have resilience is your anchor in times of uncertainty. You will also develop a resilient mind through positive thinking.

2. Resilient Body Through Healthy Living

In Barbados, the easternmost jewel of the Caribbean, the perpetual embrace of sun, sea, and sand beckons locals and visitors alike to revel in its delights. A day here is incomplete without savoring some Chefette, indulging in Oistins' fish, or perhaps enjoying a hearty platter of pudding and souse. Now, I hear you asking, "But Pastor, doesn't healthy living involve healthy eating?" Absolutely, and I encourage you to balance these delightful indulgences with nourishing choices.

Yet, resilience goes beyond just a balanced diet; it encompasses a vibrant lifestyle that melds both exercise and rest. Simple pleasures, like an early morning stroll or an afternoon walk by the historic Garrison Savannah, can be refreshing. Maybe even a heart-pumping run around the National Stadium or a serene swim at one of the island's picturesque beaches. As the famous Nike slogan encourages, "Just do it!" — initiate a lifestyle that represents your ideal balance between leisure and vitality, between work and rest.

Remember, even God took a break on the seventh day after His creation masterpiece. Unlike the tireless energizer bunny, we humans have our limits, necessitating breaks for rejuvenation and restoration. Delegate tasks when necessary, seek help when needed, and never feel guilty for prioritizing your wellbeing. Your emotional stability and physical fitness are as vital as your spiritual readiness. So, build resilience in your body!

However, in the hustle and bustle of life, many of us fall prey to the incessant urge to keep going, often neglecting the signs of weariness our bodies manifest. I, too, have walked this path, a dedicated pastor who preached the importance of rest yet failed to heed my advice. In my early 30s, amidst a Holy Communion service, my body gave a stern warning, which I sadly ignored. Overwhelmed by stress and fatigue, I collapsed, a wake-up call that came fiercely and unannounced.

To all the passionate and dedicated souls reading this, remember that resting does not diminish your commitment or intensity. Instead, it refines and replenishes your energies, allowing you to pursue your goals with renewed vigor and focus. My newfound love for the gym has taught me that building resilience is not only about repetitions and sets but also about integrating rest and nutrition conscientiously.

So, let's take a moment to pause. Yes, right now. Though the journey through these lines might be gripping, grant yourself a brief respite. Inhale deeply, filling your lungs with rejuvenating air, and then release it slowly. Repeat this calming cycle four times, immersing yourself in the symphony of sounds surrounding you, both near and far. Relax, for you are capable, resilient, and prepared to traverse the paths that lie ahead with grace and vitality.

3. Resilient Heart With Empathetic Giving

During an orientation week sermon at the University of the West Indies Cave Hill Campus, I underscored the essence of their ethos, "One fly - All soar!" For all of us to truly soar, it is paramount to foster hearts resilient in empathetic giving. This virtue can be manifested through several avenues:

A family that cares – We all have our peaks and troughs, good days and bad days, moments of grace, and others not so graceful. But it is imperative to show consistent care for each other, transcending the confines of holidays and special occasions. As John Maxwell insightfully noted, people only start to care about your knowledge when they recognize the depth of your concern for them. In these trying times, showcasing genuine care is not just virtuous but necessary.

A family that shares- Remember to extend a helping hand to those around you, especially those less fortunate. Embrace humility to both give and receive gracefully. I frequently remind my congregation that small acts can lead to monumental impacts when guided by God's hand. This sentiment is echoed in the tales of the young boy with five loaves and two fish and the widow with a mere mite - modest contributions that resonated deeply. You are blessed to be a conduit of blessings, hence share generously.

A family that bears- There are individuals amongst us who find themselves at a disadvantage, be it financial, emotional, or physical. They require our understanding and support. As a community, we must bear each other's burdens, uplifting and fortifying one another through life's trials.

In recent times, some of us witnessed devastating losses – from the death of family members to job layoffs. In 2021, the Caribbean islands faced the wrath of hurricanes, leaving many students and their families homeless. The hurdles seem endless, from stalled loans to health issues and strained family dynamics. Yet, we must rally together, bearing one another's burdens to ensure everyone crosses the finish line victoriously.

Contrary to societal teachings that advocate severing ties with those perceived as dragging us down, we should embody the spirit of unity showcased by the world's armies, whose ethos is leaving no soldier behind. This spirit demands the strong to protect the weak and the affluent to assist the impoverished.

I've always been fascinated by the 110m and the 400m hurdles races. In the 110m hurdles, challenges emerge swiftly, urging competitors to confront them with full force, a lesson imparted to me by my coach during my hurdling days. Meanwhile, the 400m hurdles represent a relentless series of obstacles from start to finish, a vivid metaphor for life's persistent trials. Despite the hurdles you encounter throughout your journey, persist, for success is attainable.

In this journey of life, resilient minds foster positive outlooks, resilient bodies encourage healthy lifestyles, and resilient hearts breed empathetic giving. This is our true essence, a beacon in the chaotic seas of uncertainty. So, anchor yourself firmly in resilience, navigating this splendid journey with grace and divine empowerment. May resilience guide you amidst the chaotic waves of uncertainty, leading you to a blessed harbor by God's grace.

Resilience - Your Anchor In Uncertainty

Ministry Encouragement

If you are a Pastor, Bishop, Apostle, Church Leader or leader in the making, this bonus chapter is for you.

I wish to share a piece of encouragement and challenge that stems from a personal and humbling experience of mine. Nineteen years after graduating from the United Theological College of the West Indies (UTCWI), I received an invitation to address the college as the speaker for their Annual Founders' Day Service. As elating as this opportunity was, it also brought along a surge of nervousness.

Imagine standing before the intellects, lecturers and mentors who once instructed you. What was most unsettling, was that I would be the first to have to preach online via **Zoom** due to the circumstances imposed by the ongoing pandemic. Yet, with all these swirling thoughts and reservations, my commitment to encourage and challenge you regarding the outlook of ministry during and post this pandemic era remains steadfast.

The theme selected for the UTCWI's Founders' Day Celebrations Worship Service on March 1, 2021 at 6:00pm, was **"Ministry in Changing Times,"** drawing inspiration from Ecclesiastes Chapter 3:1-11 and Luke Chapter 4:18-30.

Ecclesiastes 3:1-11 **"For everything there is a season, and a time for every matter under heaven:**

²a time to be born, and a time to die;
a time to plant, and a time to pluck up what is planted;
³a time to kill, and a time to heal;
a time to break down, and a time to build up;
⁴a time to weep, and a time to laugh;
a time to mourn, and a time to dance;
⁵a time to throw away stones, and a time to gather stones together;
a time to embrace, and a time to refrain from embracing;
⁶a time to seek, and a time to lose;
a time to keep, and a time to throw away;
⁷a time to tear, and a time to sew;
a time to keep silence, and a time to speak;
⁸a time to love, and a time to hate;
a time for war, and a time for peace.

The God-Given Task

⁹What gain have the workers from their toil? ¹⁰I have seen the business that God has given to everyone to be busy with. ¹¹He has made everything suitable for its time; moreover, he has put a sense of past and future into their minds, yet they cannot find out what God has done from the beginning to the end.

REV. DR. ADRIAN SMITH

Luke 4:18-19

The Spirit of the Lord is upon me,
because he has anointed me
to bring good news to the poor.
He has sent me to proclaim release to the captives
and recovery of sight to the blind,
to let the oppressed go free,
¹⁹ to proclaim the year of the Lord's favor."

The only constant in life is CHANGE. We must embrace the eternal truth that change is the sole constant dancing through the tapestry of life, echoing in the first verse, first line of the cherished hymn, "Through all the changing scenes of life." Change, swift and relentless, cascades upon the institutions and cultures carefully crafted over decades, pushing them to evolve.

Life's essence is encapsulated in change—a fact mirrored in every organization, family, and church, and celebrated in the sacred Hebrew Scriptures read tonight. Here, seasons and times ebb and flow in divine harmony, as outlined by the wise teacher, Qoheleth, signifying God's intentional design interwoven with change. The teacher, reminds us that there is a time for this, and a time for that. God has "in-built" change into His creation. Each season, whether it's a time to mourn or to dance, to break down or to build up, has its purpose and its challenges. God, in His infinite wisdom, has set these seasons, embedding in us a sense of past and future. Though we might not fully grasp His works from beginning to end, we acknowledge and move in these set times.

In navigating these waves of change, we confront challenges and confusion. We encounter digitally savvy congregants, each harboring unique worldviews and values, and we grapple with economic, political, and environmental uncertainties. In this crucible of change—marked by a leadership vacuum, global pandemics, and moral ambiguities—we ponder the essence and relevance of the Church, empathizing with leaders and clergy navigating these turbulent waters.

Amid these challenges, we observe also the rise of false prophets and impostors, sowing discord, tarnishing the reputation of devout leaders, misrepresenting the Word of God and the kingdom of God. Clearly, we cannot do business, church and ministry as usual. In these transformative times, what virtues should ministries embody and exhibit to shepherd their flock through the intricate maze of change?

1. Spirit -led Ministry - Follow God's Lead

God has not stopped speaking. God has not put the earth on auto pilot. He has not gone on furlough, study leave, sick leave or maternity leave. God is still in control. God is not dead. God's voice, tender yet steadfast, continues to guide, for He never abandons His creation. The ministry, underpinned by divine inspiration, should not resort to gimmicks or trends such as (five-steps to successful ministry, or seven secrets to doing ministry) but must be a conduit of the Holy Spirit's guidance. Ministry must be God-led, God-driven, and God-inspired. Ministry in changing times is still a Spirit-led, Spirit-infused ministry. **God's Spirit which leads, is transcending what is trending, popular, or even what is profitable.**

Amid the uncertainties, let the Spirit infuse us with courage and wisdom, guiding our steps even when the path seems daunting. For isn't it true that God's ways and thoughts soar above our understanding, as testified by the lives of Job, Jonah, Daniel, and the three Hebrew boys?

The Spirit of the Lord is upon me. The Spirit of the Lord

is upon us. **"In the last days it will be,"** God declares, **²⁸ I will pour out my Spirit upon all people. Your sons and daughters will prophesy. Your old men will dream dreams, and your young men will see visions. Joel 2:28 (NLT)**

Live by the Spirit. Walk by the Spirit. Preach by the Spirit. Teach by the Spirit. Serve by the Spirit. Is this not the encouragement of the wisdom writers? We must trust in the Lord with all our heart and lean not to our own understanding, in all our ways acknowledge God and God shall direct our path? I don't know if we still sing it or pray it, but the chorus says, *"Anointing fall on me. Let the power of the Holy Ghost fall on me*, on you, on us, on UTC, on every servant of The Most -High God.

Ministry must, ought to be, Spirit-led – Follow God's Lead

2. Liberative Ministry – Break The Cycle

It is not about being cool and fun. When people attend church, they are not just looking for information. They are looking for transformation. We are the most content-laden generation ever. People have access to more information than ever before. In a world drowning in content, the real challenge lies in the application. A ministry that fosters discipleship, engagement, and experiential faith will undoubtedly shimmer brighter than those inviting passive participation. It is an obvious but often overlooked truth that nothing changes until there is behavioural change. We must be the agents of the change we want to see. This requires a changed mind-set and changed behaviours.

Authentic change begins with transformed minds and hearts, as seen in Jesus' proclamation in Luke Chapter 4, where

He extends His hands to the marginalized, offering liberation from various societal and personal shackles. He announced that He came to liberate the impoverished, the war captives, the poor in health and the political prisoners from real oppressive structures. Jesus came to turn the economic structures upside down, instituting the Year of Jubilee, when crushing debts were forgiven and slaves were freed.

People today are still bound. They are captives and prisoners to various systems and injustices. We still have to deal with racism, oppression, generational poverty, corruption and politics in the church. We even remain captives of our own lives, when God has urged and encouraged freedom in HIM. Are we doing what He has put on our hearts and spirits to do, which may call for us to step out of our comfort zone? We should be mobilised to help free people from the captivity of alcohol, drugs, sexual sins and perversions, self-centeredness and selfishness. We should also be mobilised to step out of religious boxes and socialisations if The Holy Spirit is calling us to follow a gifting.

Scholars keep referencing this group of four:

The Poor – The homeless and malnourished

The Captives – Those who are in bondage by sin, Satan, drugs, alcoholism, pornography, gluttony, materialism, gossip, jealousy, impatience, misery, discontent, unkindness and insensitivity.

The Blind – Those with physical infirmities: genuine disabilities and illnesses, spiritual blindness.

The Oppressed – Those who cannot protect themselves: the widow, the orphan, the unborn, the children, and the abused.

Remember to look out for and stand up for those who are less fortunate than ourselves. The saints would always sing,

"I've a message from the Lord, a message full of life, full of love.
Look and live!

Or, we can sing the all too familiar:

> *Rescue the perishing, care for the dying,*
> *Snatch them in pity from sin and the grave;*
> *Weep o'er the erring one, lift up the fallen,*
> *Tell them of Jesus, the mighty to save.*

> *Refrain:*
> *Rescue the perishing, care for the dying,*
> *Jesus is merciful, Jesus will save.*

3. Compassionate ministry- love the people

Here's the truth: Before the pandemic cast its long shadow, churches were grappling with dwindling attendance and accusations of hypocrisy. In these challenging times, a symphony of voices on social media platforms echoes the yearning for genuine, God-inspired love and compassion. There are too many complaints about the lack of compassion in churches. Our very own Bishop Conrad Spencer keeps lamenting that we are very good at the cognitive but lack the affective. Authentic, loving and genuine communities are scarcer than they have ever been in our lifetime.

Amid this thirst for authentic connections, we're called to embrace empathy and soft skills, reflecting the Acts Chapter 2 and Chapter 4 model of sharing and caring. The ministry should be a sanctuary of love, offering support and understanding without judgment or expectation.

If others cannot gather can you still connect? Ministry is about people. We have to stop using people, stop manipulating people, stop abusing people, stop shaming people, and just love people. At times we fail. We only know people's numbers when we want something. We seem to care nothing about their well-being, nothing about their struggles. Again, and again it is about what we want; what we need; and how they can help us. When these people no longer possess the resources to help us- we dump them and forget about them.

In these changing times – love the people!

Put yourself in other people's shoes. You might still have a job, a home, and parents, siblings or children who are alive. Some people don't have these things.

You completed your education; some are struggling.

You didn't mess up as bad as others, but can you love the one who is messing up, still struggling, hasn't gotten it all together yet?

It is easy to love those who love you. What about loving those who don't love you? What about loving those who judge and criticise you? Are you loving them?

Where is the heart of compassion? What were Jesus' questions to Simon Peter?

15 After breakfast Jesus asked Simon Peter, "Simon son of John, do you love me more than these?[e]"

"Yes, Lord," Peter replied, "you know I love you."

"Then feed my lambs," Jesus told him.

16 Jesus repeated the question: "Simon son of John, do you love me?"

"Yes, Lord," Peter said, "you know I love you."

"Then take care of my sheep," Jesus said.

[17] A third time he asked him, "Simon son of John, do you love me?"

Peter was hurt that Jesus asked the question a third time. He said, "Lord, you know everything. You know that I love you."

Jesus said, "Then feed my sheep. John 21:15-17 (NLT)

Empathy is the connection you have with another's pain or joy. Alas, we are too quick in the church to judge and demonise rather than to empathise.

Ministry in changing times is a Spirit led, liberative ,compassionate ministry. It is also a:

4. Resilient Ministry - Don't Give Up

The eyes of all in the synagogue were fixed on Him. [21] Then He began to say to them, "Today this scripture has been fulfilled in your hearing." [22] All spoke well of Him and were amazed at the gracious words that came from His mouth. They said, "Is not this Joseph's son?"[28] When they heard this, all in the synagogue were filled with rage. [29] They got up, drove Him out of the town, and led Him to

the brow of the hill on which their town was built, so that they might hurl Him off the cliff.

In some Bibles, the heading of this portion of Scripture is labelled as, The Rejection of Jesus at Nazareth. While many people know Luke Chapter 4:18-19 and the links to Isaiah Chapter 61, it is the surrounding verses that temper, humble us and remind us amidst the admiration, whispers of skepticism and disbelief fluttered through the air, underscoring the perpetual challenge ministries face: not everyone will embrace your message, not everybody will support you.

Some doubt our relevance and the power we profess: **Is this not Joseph's son?**

Some disagree with our proclamation of truth and they are filled with rage.

Some desperately tried to stop, harm, and drive Jesus out of town. They led Him to the brow of the hill on which their town was built, so that they might hurl him off the cliff.

Resilience is the capacity and ability to recover quickly from difficulties, depression, illness and adversity. It's your ability to rebound. Some call it toughness. We cannot give up and give in easily. Try, try and keep trying!

As I reminisce about the spirited evening services of my youth, the melody of a cherished chorus, the senior women loved to sing, (and they would be beating the tambourines and dancing) was:

"I am determined to hold on to the end. Jesus is with me on Him I can depend. I know I have salvation I feel it in my soul, I am determined to hold on, hold on..."

Resilience! We are battered by storms and hurricanes every year. As a nation we may be black-listed or grey-listed by European counterparts. They may issue travel advisories which, encourage people not to travel to our country, but we are a resilient people.

A song was released in Barbados to help people cope during COVID-19. It was titled, This Is Who We Are. As the people of God, this is who we actually are: **⁸ We are pressed on every side by troubles, but we are not crushed. We are perplexed, but not driven to despair. ⁹ We are hunted down, but never abandoned by God. We get knocked down, but we are not destroyed. ¹⁰ Through suffering, our bodies continue to share in the death of Jesus so that the life of Jesus may also be seen in our bodies. 2 Corinthians 4: 8-10**

So, as Beth Lewis in a workshop encouraged us as Moravians in the Eastern West Indies, let us, Hold! Grow! Fold!

5. Innovative Ministry- Do it Differently

With the world in flux, adapting our ministries is not optional; it's imperative. If the world has changed and the people are changing, then ministry must change. If the culture is changing, then we must change our communication and communicate in the language of the culture.

In a landscape where technologies and cultural norms are continually shifting, our approach to ministry must be equally fluid and innovative, without losing sight of our core values and purpose. It is easy for us to accept that in washing clothes back in the day in Barbados we used a juking board. Today, most people use washing machines and dryers. In terms of cooking, there was the coal pot. Now we have the microwave and air-fryers. There used to be a barter system, money and cash. Now we are dealing with crypto currencies, online banking, debit and credit cards. We moved from walking, horses, chariots, cars, airplanes and boats. We now have self-driven vehicles.

Some things have to be done differently. Innovate! Innovate! We can innovate. You can innovate.

Innovation isn't synonymous with busyness or discarding foundational principles (as we proverbially say - throw out the baby with the bath water). It's a conscious, purpose-driven effort to enhance the effectiveness and reach of our ministries.

What COVID-19 has done is to strip away the busyness of life, and of the church. But the same pitfalls that needed to be avoided in the pre-COVID 19 era are still out there, though perhaps in different forms.

The means can become the end.

Busyness can replace effectiveness.

Activity can eclipse results.

Leadership in these dynamic times demands agility, adaptability, and a readiness to pivot, when necessary, always guided by faith and spiritual discernment. We are sometimes too flat footed and too reactive, too committed to a style rather than the Spirit which leads us. Get in a state of readiness. Change direction. SHIFT! It is not a sin to shift or change direction. It takes faith to change direction. It takes faith to shift, and we know it is impossible to please God without faith.

As always you will hear:

"We have never done it that way before." Let them know there is a first time for everything.

We may not always know and see everything, but we are people of faith who, walk by faith and not by sight.

It can be done. What is impossible with man is possible with God.

Our message is timeless and unchanging; the method of communicating it, and the application of it to life, must constantly change and adapt.

I recently came across a quote which reads:

"Success is moving from failure to failure without loss of enthusiasm."

You Version, a free Bible app developed by the team at Life Church, failed in its first iteration. They launched it as a website that almost nobody visited. Shortly thereafter, they relaunched it as an app. It has now been installed almost 300 million times around the world.

Urgency

Remember, innovating doesn't dilute the depth or soundness of your ministry. At its core, innovation is an enlightened practice rooted in robust teaching and continuous learning. Our commitment to adapt isn't merely about survival—it's a manifestation of our divine call to reach and resonate with a changing world with enthusiasm and hope.

For Christian leaders, while the urgency of transformation is made evident by the reality of our circumstances, the energy for transformation is inherent in our call and identity as followers of Jesus.

Now, more than ever, we find ourselves in a "changing time" — a season where resilience isn't just a virtue but a necessity. Our ministry has expanded beyond the physical walls of the church, reaching through the digital screens as we adapt to the new norm brought by the pandemic. And while this transition may seem daunting, remember the words in Luke

4:18-19. The Spirit of the Lord has anointed and appointed us for this very season to proclaim good news, bring release to captives, recovery of sight to the blind, and freedom to the oppressed.

In these unprecedented times, our resilience is tested and refined. But let it be known that our resilience isn't self-manufactured but God-given. It's the anchor that keeps us steadfast amidst the uncertainty, enabling us to navigate through the seasons of ministry with grace and strength. Let it be the force that not just helps us bounce back but also enables us to bounce forward, embracing the changing times with faith and expectancy.

As you continue to lead and shepherd the flock entrusted to you, may your heart be encouraged and your spirit be resilient. Understand that in every season, whether of plenty or of want, of joy or of sorrow, of speaking or of keeping silent, the Lord is with you, equipping and empowering you for the task at hand.

I encourage you now that you have made it to the end of this book, let the preceding thoughts be a catalyst for reflection and action, prompting you to explore and embrace the ministry God has placed on your heart, armed with knowledge and ready for growth. Amen.

End Notes

1   https://christianmusicandhymns.com/2019/09/his-eye-is-on-sparrow-story-this-song.html

2   https://www.biblestudytools.com/dictionary/providence-of-god/

3   https://www.learnreligions.com/serenity-and-recovery-prayers-700496

4   http://www.discipleshiptools.org/apps/articles/?articleid=37121&columnid=4166

5   https://www.merriam-webster.com/dictionary/abandon, https://www.dictionary.com/browse/abandon, https://www.oxfordlearnersdictionaries.com/definition/american_english/abandon_1

6   https://bible.org/article/source-true-strength

Printed in the United States
by Baker & Taylor Publisher Services